INTRODUCTION

My love of hammering wire originates from my background in metalwork jewellery. The fact that wire is so flexible and versatile yet can become tough and solid when hammered fuels my designs. It makes it possible to create beautiful, timeless jewellery for next to nothing, in no time at all. You don't need to invest in a workshop full of expensive tools and materials; just a spool of wire (yes any wire!) some pliers and wire cutters and a trusty hammer and steel block will provide you with hours of creative, therapeutic fun.

Hammering has been my personal therapy through many of life's ups and downs. As a teacher, I have also seen the benefits in others as they have bashed away their blues. In addition, of course, there is nothing to beat the sense of accomplishment you get from the creation of a new jewellery piece.

I originally trained in metalwork jewellery at the Metropolitan University, London, specialising in enamelling. In 1997 I was left with two young sons to bring up as a single parent, which spurred me on to find different avenues of income. I began teaching wire and bead classes at the local Adult Education centre, as well as exhibiting at shows and craft fairs. The wire and bead classes became very popular since they offered jewellery making without all the expensive investment. There was no soldering as everything was made with cold connections, giving instant fun and creative gratification.

Once I started teaching, I realised that there was no end to the design variations and permutations that I could doodle and create. I was hooked! I began experimenting with all types of wire to create one-off jewellery pieces, wedding tiaras, home décor and wire embellishments for every occasion and place.

This led to my contributing designs to US and UK magazines over the years, writing eight project books on wire and beaded jewellery and making three DVDs, and I became a demonstrator on Create & Craft TV, sponsored by Beads Direct.

I am also the creator of the Whammer, a three-in-one hammer specifically designed for wirework. In all the years of teaching and designing wire art, I had collected a variety of metalwork and jewellery hammers, all of which had long handles, much more suited to bashing out sheet metal. My pupils kept asking, 'What's the best hammer for wire?' In the end, I designed one. You don't need a Whammer to create the projects in this book, as alternatives are suggested, but obviously, it will help. Each chapter is designed to inspire a new hammering technique, from spreading wire in the first section, 'Feathers', to work-hardening in 'Shapes' and compressing in 'Scrunched Wire'. You are then let loose to combine all the skills you have learned in the last chapter 'Get Creative', where you can let your creative juices flow. Happy hammering!

HAMMERED WIRE JEWELLERY

Linda Jones

SEARCH PRESS

CONTENTS

First published in Great Britain 2016

Search Press Limited
Wellwood, North Farm Road,
Tunbridge Wells, Kent TN2 3DR

Illustrations and text copyright © Linda Jones, 2016

Photographs by Paul Bricknell at Search Press Studios

Photographs and design copyright © Search Press Ltd. 2016

ISBN: 978-1-78221-298-0

The Publishers and author can accept no responsibility for any consequences arising from the information, advice or instructions given in this publication.

Suppliers
If you have difficulty in obtaining any of the materials and equipment mentioned in this book, then please visit the Search Press website for details of suppliers:
www.searchpress.com

You are invited to visit the author's website and blog:
www.wirejewellery.co.uk
www.wireworkersguild.blogspot.com

Printed in China

Acknowledgements

I'm immensely grateful to Search Press for giving me the opportunity to produce this book of projects and allowing me creative freedom in the style and layout throughout. I'm particularly grateful to Sophie Kersey for her superb editing and support and to Paul Bricknell for his sublime photography.

Also thanks to Emily Dobson, Lin Chan and Katrina Hindley for modelling the jewellery.

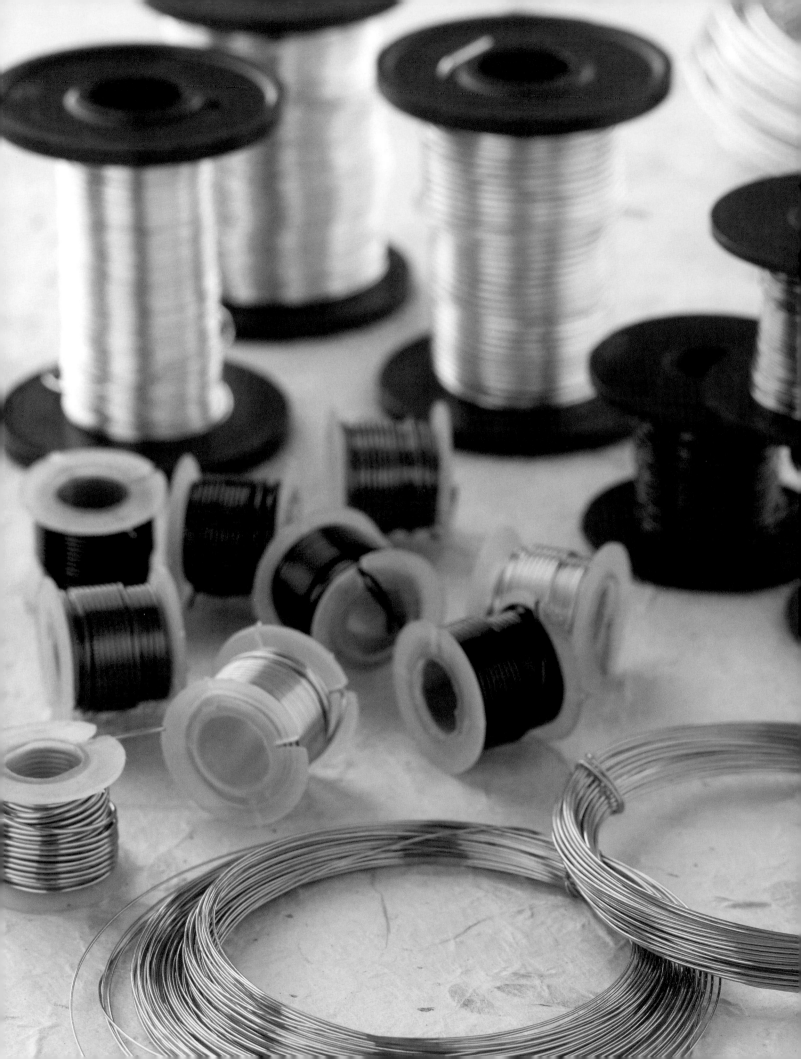

MATERIALS

One of the joys of making wire and bead jewellery is that you can start off with very few specialist tools and materials, and they are all readily available from craft outlets and online jewellery suppliers.

WIRE

This is available in many thicknesses (gauges), types (metals) and every colour of the rainbow. Initially it can be a little daunting not knowing what to purchase and where from. Craft and hobby stores as well as online bead suppliers sell spools of pre-measured lengths, while precious wires (such as platinum, gold and silver) can be purchased by length, the price being calculated by weight.

Coloured wires are usually copper-based, but can be aluminium. Generally speaking, aluminium wires can be a little too soft for the wear and tear of jewellery designs, but great for general craftwork.

The black wire used in the Doodle Dangle Choker (Page 64) is iron wire, which is not very malleable, but very resilient to hammering, and has a rustic quality that suits a lot of the project styles within this book.

The majority of the projects in this book have been created out of copper-based wires, which are less expensive and will not tarnish as quickly as sterling silver. If you wish to use sterling silver wires instead, store them in a sealed container or bag, to prevent tarnishing (although a dip into a silver cleaning solution will instantly bring back their original sparkle).

The following chart shows which wires to use for which purposes:

WIRE CHART	
26-gauge (0.4mm)	Use for binding, scrunching, knitting, weaving
22-gauge (0.6mm)	Use for threading small beads, binding and twisting
20-gauge (0.8mm)	Use for all general-purpose jewellery making
18-gauge (1mm)	Use for chunkier pieces, frames and ring shanks
16-gauge (1.25mm)	Use for chunky, bold, statement pieces and bangle frames
14-gauge (1.5mm)	
12-gauge (2mm)	

FINDINGS

Findings are the components used to join jewellery, such as clasps, earring wires, bails, jump rings, headpins. These can be bought ready-made from most craft and bead shops, but it is possible to create your own with wire. In the Basic Techniques section on page 138 you can learn how to create your own jump rings, bead links, headpins and fish-hook clasps and eyes.

Most of the projects can be adapted into various types of jewellery, so what you need depends on what you choose to make, but you might need ready-made chains, cord, bag charm clips, key ring findings, brooch backs and earring wires.

Tip

Note that items such as clasps and jump rings are not listed in the You will need lists with the projects, as there are instructions for making these in the Basic Techniques chapter (page 138).

Chains, cord, bag charm clip, key ring finding, brooch backs, clasps, jump rings and earring wires.

BEADS

From traditional pearls and semi-precious stones to sparkling iridescent crystals, as well as metal and wood beads and stone chips, there are so many to pick and choose from. Consider your colour palette before you begin making a piece – you will find plenty of inspiration for colour combinations on the internet, as well as from nature all around you. I have used a variety of semi-precious stones and glass beads, so just dip into your stash or use beads from broken necklaces to add colour and accent to your jewellery pieces.

Clockwise from top left: bail-making pliers, mandrel, ring mandrel, steel block, cone-making tool with fittings, flat-nosed, round-nosed and chain-nosed pliers and wire cutters.

TOOLS

HAMMERS

The star tool in this book is obviously the hammer!
Each project will demonstrate its
use in flattening, toughening, spreading
and compressing wire to create a
professional finish.

Specialty jewellery hammers are generally lighter
than household hammers, but you can use ANY
hammer as long as one end has a flat, smooth,
polished surface.

I would obviously recommend the Whammer
hammer, which I created for wirework, as it is
specifically weighted and will provide the very best
results. The Whammer is three hammers in one, as it has
a steel planishing head for spreading and work-hardening; a
nylon end for flattening, removing kinks and compressing wire
(especially colour-coated wire); and an interchangeable dapping
end for texturing.

The Whammer with the nylon and planishing heads fitted and dapping head on the side.

However, silversmithing hammers such as planishing or chasing are
perfectly adequate for all the projects in this book and it is also possible
to purchase nylon-headed mallets and ball pein hammers to provide extra surface texture.

STEEL BLOCK

Flat polished steel stakes or blocks can be purchased from specialty jewellery suppliers and are used
in conjunction with the hammer. Any flat piece of steel can be used, provided that the surface has no
bumps or abrasive marks, as these will be picked up on the wire surface.

MANDRELS

Ring mandrels are available from speciality jewellery stores. These tapered cone shapes are usually
marked with ring sizes. I would advise getting a steel-based one, rather than a wooden one. However,
you can create simple, one-off rings by wrapping wire around any cylindrical rod, such as a lipstick case
or marker pen. This should be slightly smaller in diameter than your ring size, as wire can spring open
slightly when removed from the mandrel. A cone-making tool is useful for making cyclone shapes in wire,
but you could use any small cone shape such as a piping nozzle.

PLIERS

Round-nosed pliers are needed to form circles, curls and coils; flat-nosed pliers to hold and bend wire
into angles; and chain-nosed pliers to grip wire and get into smaller areas as well as neaten ends. You
need all three of these for all the projects. Bail-making pliers are just cylindrical mandrels on handles,
which come with different diameter rods. I particularly like using the 6mm/8mm (¼in/⁵⁄₁₆in) ones to get
even-shaped coils and to make jump rings, links and of course bails for pendants.

WIRE CUTTERS

There are many types of cutter on the market, but I find side cutters to be the most useful type for
wirework. These have small, tapered ends that can cut into small spaces. I recommend that you purchase
the very best you can afford to avoid spiky ends that can scratch and snag on skin and clothing.

HAMMERING WIRE

Why do you need to hammer? Well, apart from the obvious aesthetic quality that it brings to your designs, it also provides structure, texture, form and an element of toughness, to enable your jewellery pieces to be durable and stand up to long-term wear and tear.

This technique has to be acquired and takes a little practice! It is not simply a bashing movement (like hammering a nail into a block of wood), but more of a 'stroking' movement, bringing the middle (or slightly convex part of the hammer) down at 90 degrees to the piece and pushing it out. To begin with, try hammering your piece standing up, so that the hammer head hits the wire squarely, rather than at an angle, which can create unwanted texture marks on the surface. After several light strokes, you will see the wire flattening and spreading and you can increase the blow in any direction to push the metal out further. The metal will also toughen (or work harden) during this process.

Hammering is also the most therapeutic technique in wirework – you can bash away all your troubles to a primitive jungle beat!

1 Place your wire shape on the steel block ready for hammering.

2 With the steel planishing head on the Whammer, or with a planishing hammer, flatten and work harden the wire shape. Hold it down with your finger and work area by area.

The hammered wire shape.

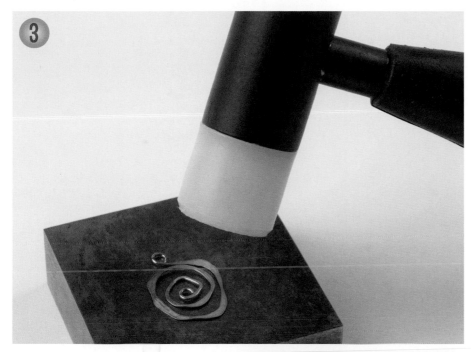

3 Flatten the piece further by hammering with a nylon head. This doesn't texture or change the shape of the wire, or lift the coating.

4 Use the dapping head to add texture. If this warps the shape, you can use the nylon head again, which will flatten the piece without affecting the texture.

The hammered, textured wire shape.

FEATHERS

Hammering metal to flatten and spread it is an ancient art, so follow in your ancestors' footsteps to create your own unique jewellery pieces. If you are a complete beginner, all it takes is a little practice to become proficient at this technique. It is a stroking rather than bashing movement that will provide the best results, flattening the wire into feather shapes, as shown in these six projects.

TRIBAL FEATHERS NECKLACE

This is a striking piece that will get the wearer noticed. It has a timeless, tribal feel and can be made in a mixture of different wires: copper, gold and silver blend, but for me, silver always wins the day.

You will need

0.8mm and 1.25mm silver-plated copper wire

2 x 8mm antique silver-plated beads

Silver-plated chain

Round-, flat- and chain-nosed pliers

Wire cutters

Hammer and steel block

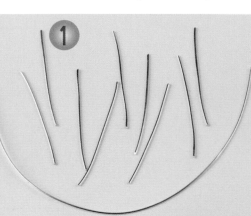

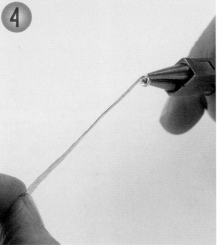

1 Begin by cutting approximately 20cm (8in) of 1.25mm wire. Retain the natural curve in the wire, as this will become the central part of the necklace to suspend all the silver 'feathers' from. Straighten out more wire from the spool and cut nine 5cm (2in) lengths.

2 Place each of the 5cm (2in) wire lengths on your steel block and begin by gently flattening the very end of each one. Increase the strength of each blow, stroking the wire down to the end, to enable it to mushroom out. If your wire seems to be spreading too much in one direction, stroke-hammer it out on the opposite side to keep it as even as possible.

3 Once you have hammered and spread one end of each of the nine wires, take the longest one (as this will be the centrepiece) and hammer the opposite end until it flattens slightly.

4 Use the tips of your round-nosed pliers to create a small link with the flattened end.

5 Thread the top link of your 'feather' onto your curved wire and position it at the centre of the curve. Take each of the remaining eight wires and trim the unhammered ends so that they are very gently graded in size, with two of each size, to create a symmetrical necklace. Repeat step 4, hammering the ends to create top links and position each of the 'feathers' on either side of the central one.

18

6 Once you've established making the centre of your necklace in this way, continue to cut slightly shorter lengths of 1.25mm wire to create more wire 'feathers', following all the steps above to expand the necklace. I used about fifty-one 'feathers' in all, but if you wish to create fewer or more, follow your creative instincts.

7 Thread your chosen beads onto each side of the necklace to keep the wire 'feathers' in place and using your round-nosed pliers, create a link at either end of the curved wire.

8 Measure the overall length required for the necklace to ascertain how much chain is required on each side. Cut these lengths and attach to each side with jump rings made from 0.8mm wire (see page 138).

9 Finally, connect a fish-hook clasp created out of 1.25mm wire (see page 141) to the ends of the chain.

Opposite:
Create a different version using 1.25mm copper wire, combined with gold-plated chain and beads.

The finished necklace.

SPLIT RING

Here's a nice simple project that can be quickly created to match a favourite outfit. If you don't have a ring mandrel, you can still create rings using lipstick cases, chunky pens or any cylindrical shape that is just slightly smaller than your actual ring size.

You will need

0.4mm and 1.25mm silver-plated copper wire

'Baroque' freshwater pearl bead

Round-, flat- and chain-nosed pliers

Wire cutters

Ring mandrel

Hammer and steel block

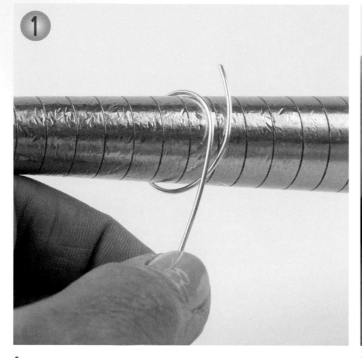

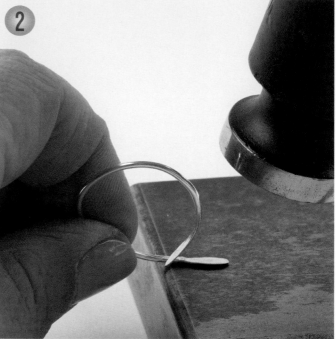

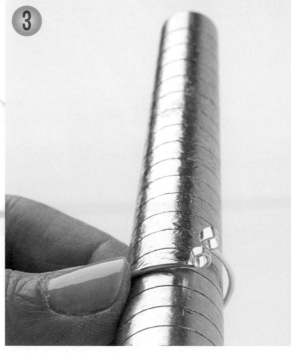

1 Working from a spool of 1.25mm wire, wrap the end around your ring mandrel, just below the ring size you require (as the wire will spring open slightly). Cut the wire from the spool, with an overlap of approximately 1cm (½in) from where the wire crosses over.

2 Using your fingers, twist the circle open to access each end and hammer to flatten and spread on a steel block.

3 Using the very tips of your round-nosed pliers, create a small link at either end of your flattened wire, curving away from the ring in the opposite direction. Replace the ring on your mandrel to reshape and resize it.

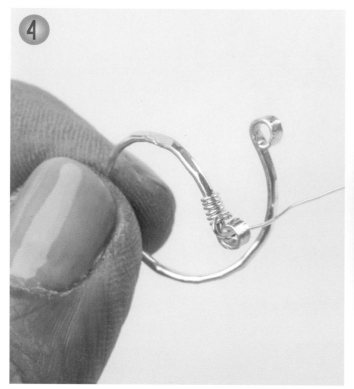

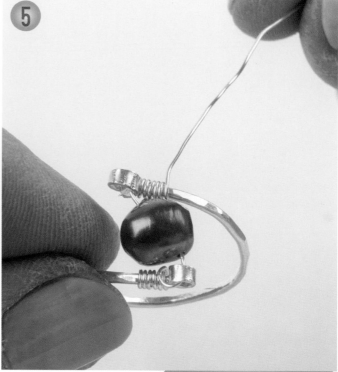

4 Cut about 7.5cm (3in) of 0.4mm wire and begin by securing it around the ring base, just by one of the links. Feed the wire through the link.

5 Add your bead or selection of small beads and wrap the wire round the opposite side of the ring. Cut off any excess and neaten the end using the tips of your chain-nosed pliers.

Tip

For a weathered look, place the ring on the mandrel and use the dapping end of the hammer to tap out a few texture dents.

Above and opposite

Have fun creating a variety of rings using pearls, faceted crystals and semi-precious stone chips.

HINGED LINKS

Unique, handmade chains always look pretty and in vogue. Once you have mastered the technique to make one link, you'll be in production. For a daintier, more delicate piece, have a go at making this bracelet with 0.8mm wire instead of 1mm.

You will need

1mm silver-plated copper wire
10 x 6mm leopard-skin agate beads
Round-, flat- and chain-nosed pliers
Wire cutters
Hammer and steel block

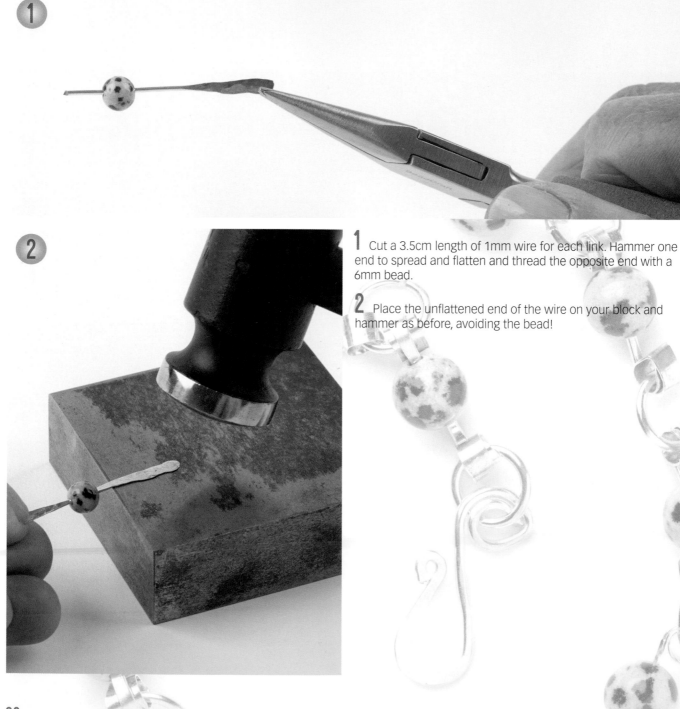

1

1 Cut a 3.5cm length of 1mm wire for each link. Hammer one end to spread and flatten and thread the opposite end with a 6mm bead.

2

2 Place the unflattened end of the wire on your block and hammer as before, avoiding the bead!

3 Using the tips of your round-nosed pliers, curl the flattened ends into small links, bringing the wire around in one direction on one side and in the other on the opposite end.

4 Create jump rings to join the bead links together as a chain and attach a clasp at the end (see pages 138–143).

The finished bracelet.

Make necklaces, bracelets and even earrings using this technique. I used frosted agate beads for the necklace and an assortment of glass and purple pearl beads for the bracelet.

STICKS & STONES PENDANT

This pendant can be scaled up or down, depending on the size stones you wish to place at the centre. If you are making a smaller version or matching earrings, I would advise using 0.8mm wire for the framework.

You will need

0.4mm and 1.25mm copper wire

Sea-glass nugget bead, aquamarine chips and freshwater pearl beads

Cord

Round-, flat- and chain-nosed pliers

Wire cutters

Hammer and steel block

1 Begin by cutting three pieces of 1.25mm wire: one 6.5cm (2½in) and two 7.5cm (3in). Curve these wires by bending them around a bottle or jar and hammer the ends on a steel block until they splay out into paddle shapes.

2 Cut three 12.7cm (5in) lengths of 0.4mm wire and use these to secure the paddle shapes where they cross over each other, leaving any leftover wire to be spiralled and flattened over the wraps.

3 Spiral any leftover wire by curling it round the round-nosed pliers, then gripping the curl in the flat-nosed pliers and turning it as shown. When all the excess wire is in the spiral, flatten it against the wrap with the flat-nosed pliers.

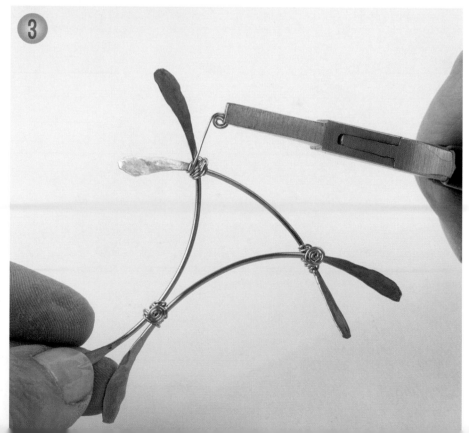

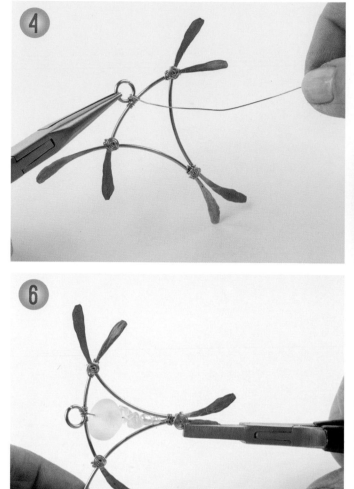

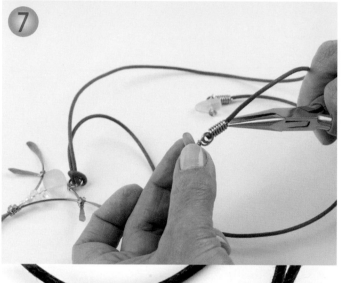

4 Cut approximately 17.8cm (7in) of 0.4mm wire and use this to bind a jump ring to the centre top of the pendant.

5 Bring the binding wire down the middle space of the pendant and thread on your chosen stone and beads to fill the space.

6 Secure the end of the wire at the bottom join of the pendant and any leftover wire can be spiralled and flattened to hide the wrap.

7 For a variable height, tie-end necklace, create two coils with links (like making jump rings, see page 138) and squeeze the last ring of each of the coils tightly around the cord ends (a tiny dab of glue will provide extra security). Attach and suspend the ends of the coils with matching beads, creating headpins at the ends (see page 140) so that you have a back detail when the necklace is worn.

The finished pendant.

Use silver-plated copper wire, semi-precious stone beads and chain for a different look (see above). You could also make a birthstone necklace for a friend or member of the family. This one (left) is an amethyst nugget, which is the birthstone for February.

SUN SCARF SLIDE

The beauty of this scarf slide is that it can be slipped on to a variety of long scarves of your choice, creating a decorative pendant to jazz up any of your outfits, whether they are casual or smart. It makes a gorgeous gift with a scarf if you create it with beads to match, or you can slip it on a chain and wear it as a necklace.

You will need

0.8mm, 1.25mm and 0.4mm silver-plated copper wire

Mixed green glass beads and bicone crystals (from seed beads to 6mm sizes) and 4mm and 6mm silver beads

1cm (½in), 3cm (1¼in) and 4cm (1½in) mandrels

Round-, flat- and chain-nosed pliers

Wire cutters

Hammer and steel block

To wear

Thread the end of your scarf through the coil, pulling it along to the centre of the scarf. Wear it like a necklace pendant, crossing each of the ends of the scarf around your neck, so that they fall on either side of the pendant.

1 Working from a spool of 0.8mm wire, wrap three to four times around the smaller 1cm (½in) mandrel to create even-sized coils, then cut from the spool leaving a projecting end of about 15cm (6in).

2 Wrap the projecting wire around all the coils in a random fashion, pulling the wire tight to avoid leaving gaps.

3 Place the wrapped circular unit on a steel block and hammer until the wires are flattened and compacted.

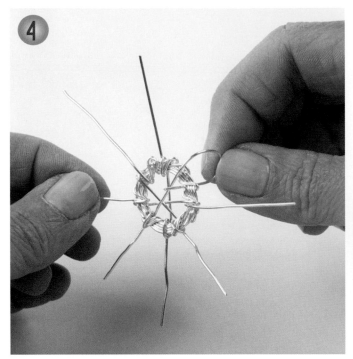

4 Cut four 10cm (4in) lengths of 0.8mm wire and attach each one across the centre of the circular unit as shown, wrapping the wire round each side to secure it.

5 Once the wires are fixed in a criss-cross fashion, trim all the projecting ends to about 3cm (1¼in) and hammer each one on a steel block to spread and flatten them.

6 Wrap the end of a length of 1.25mm wire tightly around a 4cm (1½in) circular mandrel, to form a circular frame. Cut from the spool.

7 Place the sun pendant frame at the centre of the circle and trim the hammered ends as required. Secure the frame in place by folding the ends over the edge of the circular frame.

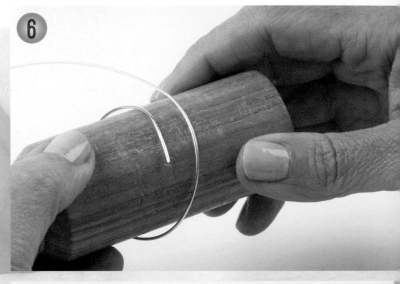

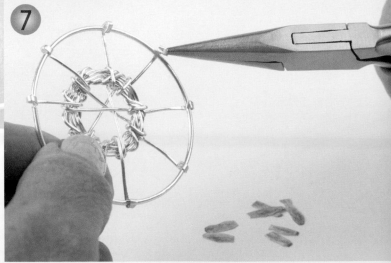

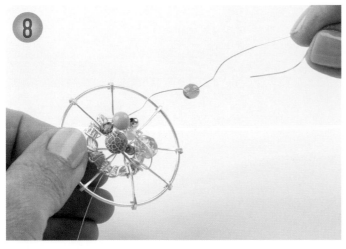

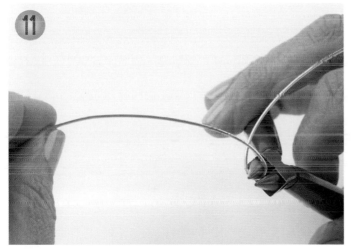

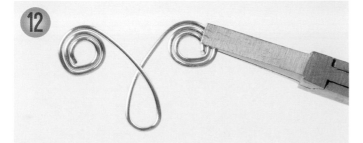

8 Cut approx. 40.5cm (16in) of 0.4mm wire and thread it with your chosen beads, attaching and securing them to fill the circular centre space with colour. Cut off any excess wire and neaten the ends.

9 To develop the project into a scarf pendant, wrap 1mm or 1.25mm wire around a circular mandrel large enough for your chosen scarf to feed through, and create an even-sized coil of approximately eight to ten complete rings. Cut from the spool.

10 Using your round-nosed pliers, create circular links at each end of the coil, positioning them at 90 degrees as shown. Spiral the wire around a few times (see step 3, page 28) until the links are aligned at the same level on either side of the coil.

11 Create a hanger by cutting 15cm (6in) of 1mm or 1.25mm wire and placing your round nosed pliers at the centre of the length. Cross the wires over on each side as shown. Hammer the hanger, but avoid hammering the part where the wires cross, as this would weaken the wires.

12 Create a circular spiral on each projecting end (see step 3, page 28).

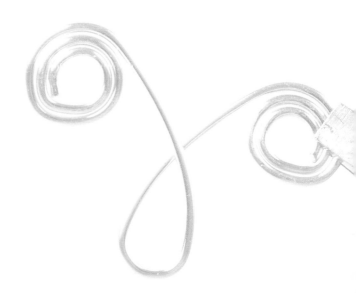

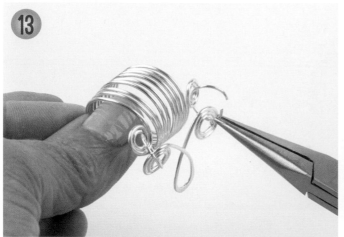

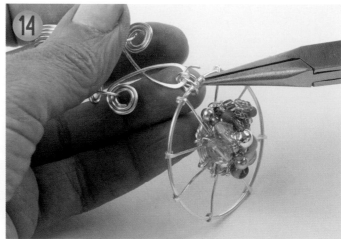

13 Use two jump rings to attach the coil to the hanger.

14 Use three jump rings to attach the sun pendant to the central loop of the hanger.

A pink aluminium 2mm wire version with assorted pearls and crystal beads

A silver-plated wire frame with a blend of turquoise, orange, red and silver beads in the centre.

This animal-print scarf looks great with a matching pendant, created out of 0.9mm black iron wire with wood and glass beads and a feature pearl to complement the scarf colours.

NOUGHTS & CROSSES PENDANT

This design is a personal favourite of mine – a reminder of a childhood game, also known as Tic Tac Toe. It can include birthstone beads, pearls, shells and even jump rings for the noughts, and crosses can be wired into the gaps. Once you have made the grid, have fun adding whatever you wish to your piece.

You will need

0.4mm. 0.8mm and 1.25mm silver-plated copper wire

Golden yellow crystal glass and 8mm pearl beads

Antique silver butterfly charm bead

Round-, flat- and chain-nosed pliers

Wire cutters

Cord

Hammer and steel block

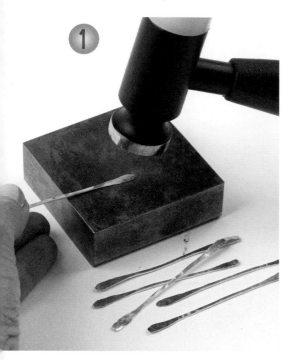

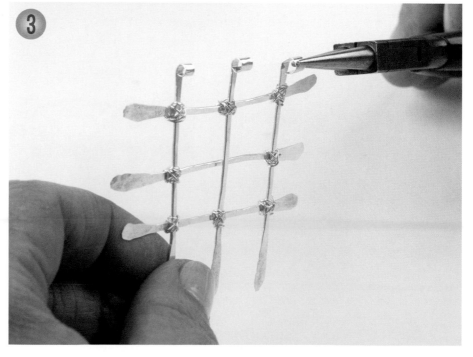

1 Begin by cutting six 5cm (2in) lengths of 1.25mm wire, or shorter if you prefer a smaller pendant. Place each of the wires on your steel block and hammer to flatten, spreading the ends out into 'paddle' shapes.

2 Cut six 7.5cm (3in) lengths of 0.4mm wire and use this to bind the paddle shapes together to form a grid. Cut off any excess wire and neaten the ends with your chain-nosed pliers.

3 Using the tips of your round-nosed pliers, create small links at the tops of the three vertical hammered wires.

40

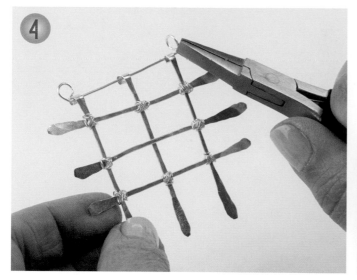

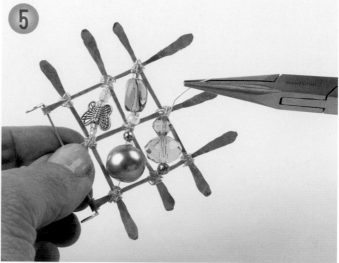

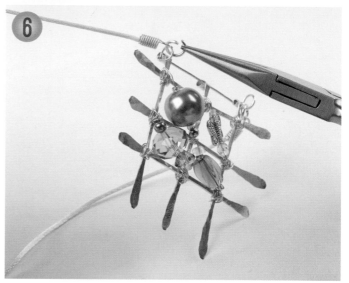

4 Cut approximately 6.5cm (2½in) of 0.8mm wire and thread this through the three top links, creating a loop on either side with round-nosed pliers. Using flat-nosed pliers, twist the links 90 degrees to the frame on each side.

5 Cut a length of 0.4mm wire and use this to secure beads in all, or just a few of the grid spaces. Wind the wire round the joins to secure it.

6 Suspend the pendant from a handmade chain or cord of your choice. Create two jump rings out of 0.8mm wire (see page 138). Connect to a cord with coils, crimping the ends as on page 32, step 7).

The finished pendant.

Create wire-framed pendants in different colours, using a selection of beads to fill the gaps. Here I have used silver-plated copper wire, ready-made chain and a few hand-forged jump ring links (see page 46).

SHAPES

One of the great things about wire is that you can endlessly doodle free-style forms that will hold their shape, especially when hammered. You could start with a very simple circle of wire (or jump ring) as in the Ring Chain Bracelet and move on to curves and wiggles as in the Cleopatra's Collar and Scalloped Necklace projects. Once you have mastered the techniques in this chapter, you will realise that you can draw any framework in wire and fix it into shape by hammering, linking or binding.

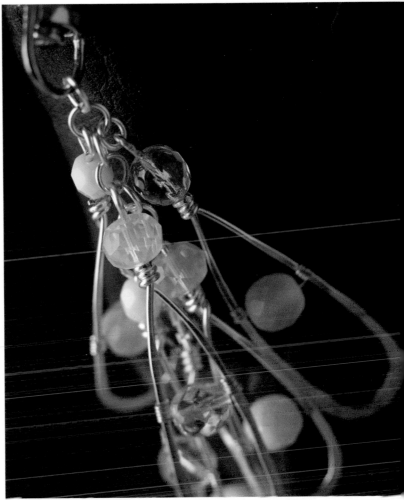

RING CHAIN BRACELET

The simplest and humblest of chain links can look so effective when hammered, as each unit takes on a unique handmade characteristic. Colour can be introduced by wiring in some beads if desired. This style will also suit necklaces and matching earring designs.

You will need

0.4mm and 1mm brass wire

Small sodalite nugget beads and blue seed beads

Round-, flat- and chain-nosed pliers

Wire cutters

Bail-making pliers, 6mm and 8mm (¼in and ⁵⁄₁₆in)

Hammer and steel block

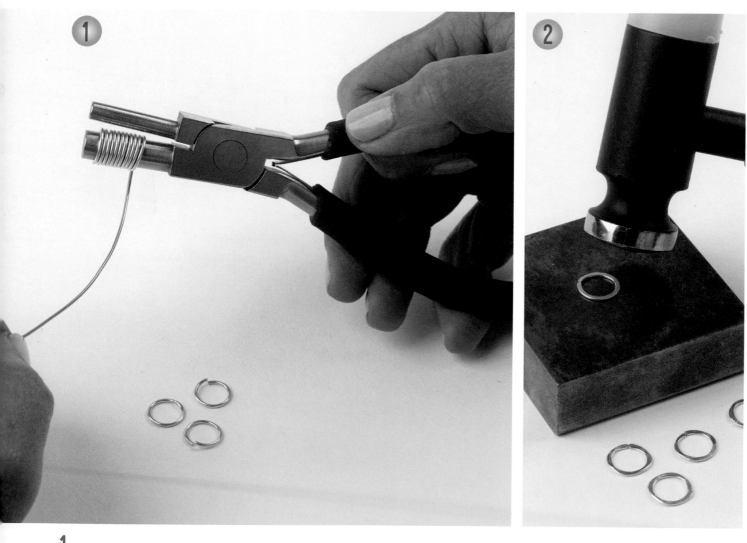

1 Create eighteen circular links by wrapping 1mm wire around the 8mm (⁵⁄₁₆in) bail-making pliers (refer to the instructions for making jump rings on page 138). If you don't have bail-making pliers, you can also use a chunky marker pen.

2 Hammer nine of the links in four areas and ensure that the ends meet.

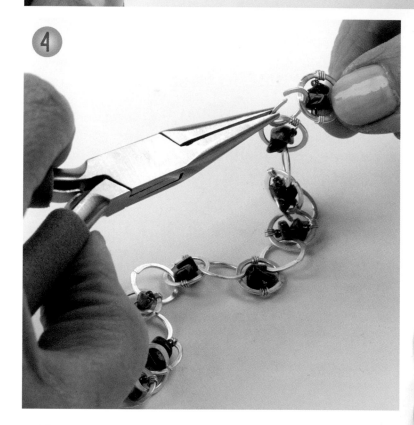

3 Cut a short length of 0.4mm wire and attach it to each of the nine hammered links. Wind it round one edge, thread on sodalite nugget beads and blue seed beads, take the wire across the centre and secure it on the opposite side. Trim and neaten the ends with the tips of your chain-nosed pliers.

4 Create a continuous chain by connecting a bead link to an un-hammered jump ring link, alternating as you go.

5 Create a toggle or fish-hook clasp for the ends and attach using jump rings.

The finished bracelet.

This silver wire ring chain bracelet has amethyst chip beads and earrings to match.

This version of the ring chain bracelet features bronze wire with faceted burgundy-dyed quartz beads.

CLEOPATRA'S COLLAR

This might look complicated, but it is based on pure repetition of shape. If you are worried about keeping the wiggles looking even, you could create them on a jig, but in my book, anything slightly wonky adds to the originality of a piece!

You will need

0.4mm and 0.8mm silver-plated copper wire

1 x 8mm and 2 x 4mm Czech glass crystal beads

Round-, flat- and chain-nosed pliers

Wire cutters

Hammer and steel block

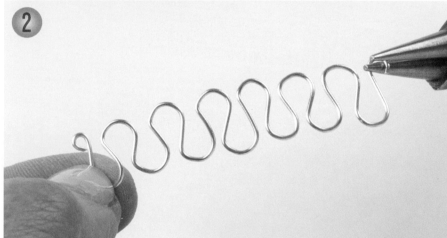

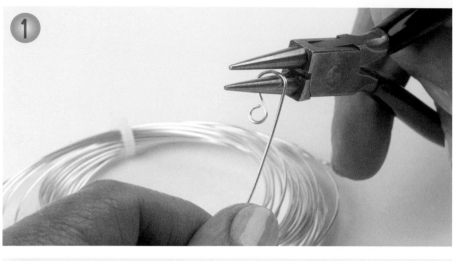

1 Working from the end of a spool of 0.8mm wire, create a small link using your round-nosed pliers. Place the widest part of the pliers next to this link and bring the wire around to form the first loop (or 'wiggle').

2 Continue curving the wire around your round-nosed pliers to form a unit of about seven to nine even-sized wiggles. Using the tips of your pliers, create a small link at the end of the unit, in line with the first at the opposite end. Repeat to create five more units.

3 Create the centrepiece unit with a larger and longer central loop (to fit your focal bead).

4 Hammer all the rounded ends of the units.

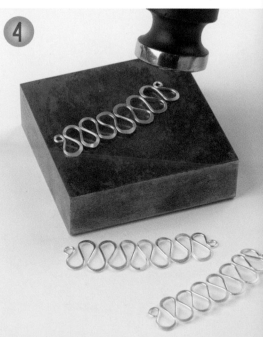

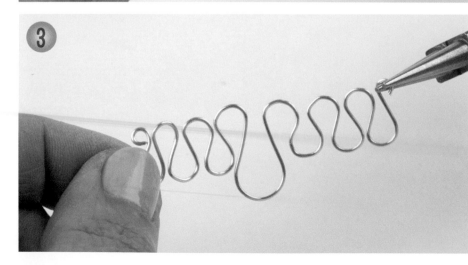

5 Cut a small length of 0.4mm wire and use this to securely bind your chosen beads to the centre of the larger loop.

6 Connect three of the units to each side of the centrepiece with jump rings and finish the collar by attaching a fish-hook clasp at the very end. Spend a little time adjusting each unit so that the wiggles sit close together without any gaps. You can also gently mould them over a curved mandrel so that they sit well around the neck.

tip

Experiment by making a chunkier collar with thicker wire, such as 1mm or 1.25mm. You can also choose to make it more colourful by filling more of the gaps with wired-on beads.

The finished collar with matching earrings (see page 122 for Cleo's Earrings).

Opposite

A really striking statement necklace can be created by linking the units in descending rows and attaching decorative beads to suspend at the end.

FLOWER BROOCH

This decorative piece can be created for a hair accessory, or wired on to a plant stick or anything that you wish to embellish. As with all the projects in the book, you can scale it up or down by using different gauges and lengths of wire.

You will need

0.8mm copper and silver-plated copper wire, 0.4mm silver-plated copper wire

Assorted semi-precious stone chip beads: turquoise, malachite and tiger's eye

Round- and chain-nosed pliers

Bail-making pliers, 6mm and 8mm (¼in and 5/16in) or round mandrel such as a pen or pencil

Wire cutters

Hammer and steel block

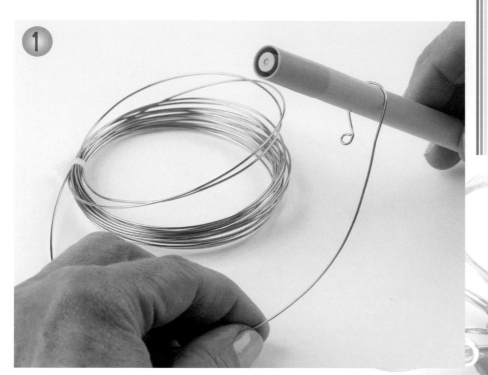

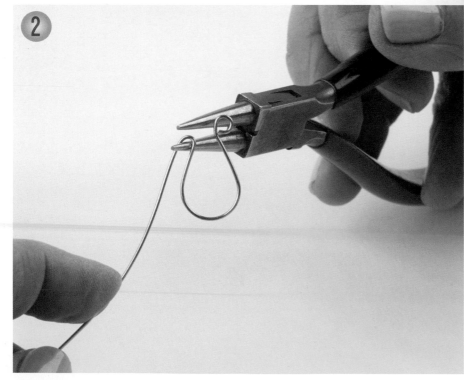

1 Working from a spool of 0.8mm wire, use the tips of your round-nosed pliers to create a small link. Place your cylindrical mandrel (I used a pen) approximately 2.5cm (1in) up from the link and bend the wire around to form a loop. This is your first petal.

2 Using the tips of your round-nosed pliers, bend the wire back in the opposite direction.

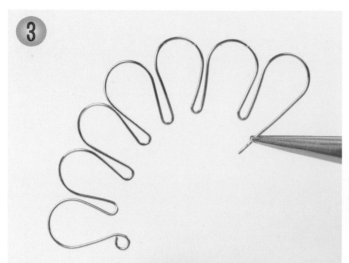

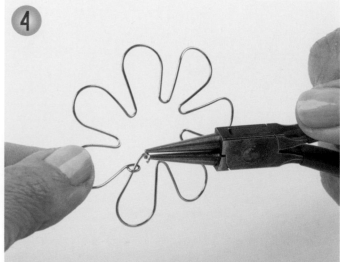

3 Create six more petals in the same way, so that you have seven in total. Cut the wire from the spool (leaving just enough to form a link).

4 Pull the petal loops around to form a circle and post the cut end through the small link (created in step1) to secure the frame together.

5 Repeat all the steps to create another flower frame in 0.8mm silver-plated wire, making it with slightly shorter petals. Hammer the ends of all the petals on a steel block to flatten and work-harden them.

6 Working from the end of your 0.8mm silver spool, create a small link with your round-nosed pliers. Bend the wire up and down on your pliers to create seven narrow zigzags about 1.5cm (⁵⁄₈in) in height, and cut from the spool.

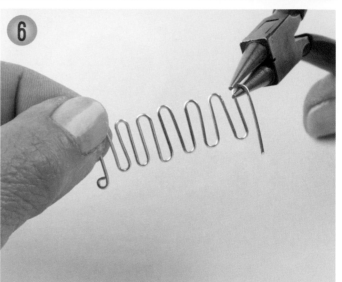

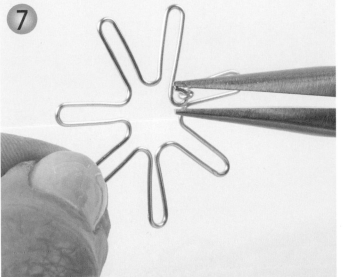

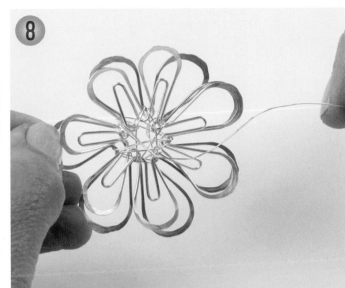

7 Pull the zigzag frame around to form a circle and secure by attaching the cut end through the small link.

8 Stack all three frames on top of each other (with the zigzag unit from step 6 at the very top) and using about 30cm (12in) of 0.4mm silver-plated wire, bind the three layers around their centres to secure them as one. Once all the frames are firmly attached, bring the ends of the 0.4mm wire around to the back of the flower and twist together.

9 Use the projecting wire to secure your choice of beads to the centre of the flower frame, covering all your binding underneath. 'Sew' in as many beads as you wish to fill the centre of the frame. Cut off any projecting wire and neaten the ends.

10 You can use the tips of your round-nosed pliers to bend the very tips of your zigzag frame in towards the central beaded area.

Tip
Your flower is now ready to be attached to a brooch back, suspended from a cord or chain or attached to a hair grip. You could also create a smaller version to wire onto a ring shank.

A flower necklace created out of bronze and brass wire, with a wire pom-pom centre. It is threaded with 4mm faceted brown crystals and attached to a brown cotton cord.

Opposite
This amethyst chip bead choker is threaded onto nylon filament. The bronze and silver wire flower has a centre created from amethyst chips and a burgundy faceted quartz feature bead. The flower is placed off-centre for an asymmetrical look.

PETAL BUNCH CASCADE

Here's another project with lots of therapeutic hammering fun! If you prefer something other than a handbag charm, you could make a key ring or pendant. Matching bunched earrings can look dramatic and dressy, or just use a single petal drop to make an elegant pair of earrings.

You will need

1mm and 0.5mm silver-plated copper wire
8mm and 10mm Czech glass beads
Bag charm clip
Round-, flat- and chain-nosed pliers
Wire cutters
Hammer and steel block

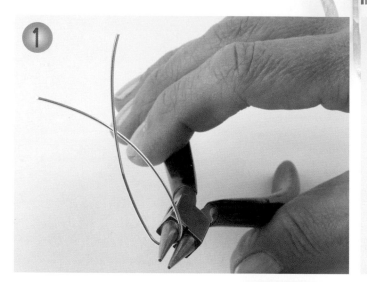

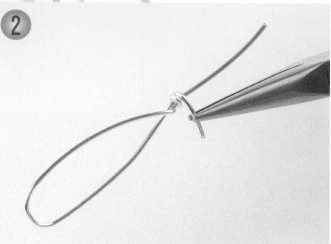

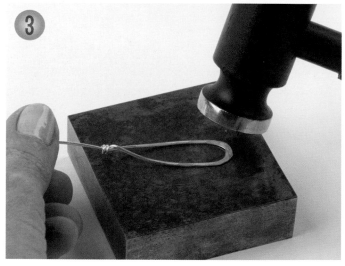

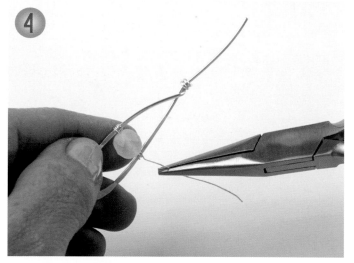

1 Cut approximately 12.5cm (5in) of 1mm wire. Place your round-nosed pliers near the centre of the length and bend around to form a loop.

2 Wrap one wire around the other to secure. Cut off any excess from the wrap and neaten the end.

3 Place the looped unit on a steel block and hammer, concentrating on the rounded end.

4 Cut 7.5cm (3in) of 0.5mm wire and wrap it on either side of the loop frame, securing a bead in the middle.

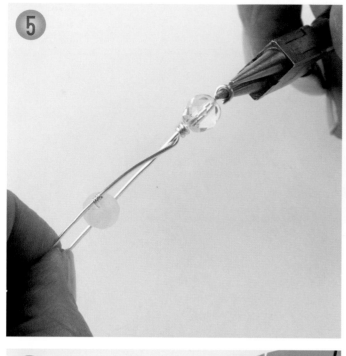

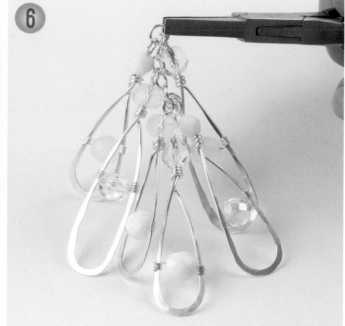

5 Thread the projecting wire at the top of the loop with your chosen bead, and using your round-nosed pliers, create a link above the bead.

6 Create at least four to six more units following steps 1–5, and attach them together with a chain of jump rings to form a bunched cascade.

7 Connect to a bag charm clip to complete the handbag charm.

The finished handbag charm.

This petal bunch design has gold wire petal shapes threaded with oval red aventurine beads, attached to dark brown cord.

A silver wire and chain necklace with frosted agate beads in blue, pink, white and black. Matching earrings complete the set.

DOODLE DANGLE CHOKER

Let your imagination take over your pliers when shaping these free-style wire doodles! You could create a matching bangle using shorter dangles. Every necklace or bangle you make with this fun technique will be a one-off. I think the dangles on this one have the look of talismanic symbols.

You will need

1mm black iron wire

Assorted antique silver-plated beads

Round-, flat- and chain-nosed pliers

Wire cutters

Large circular mandrel such as a bottle or jar

Hammer and steel block

1 Working from a spool of 1mm black iron wire, use about 5cm (2in) to form a small open spiral using your round-nosed pliers.

2 Place your pliers about 1cm (½in) along from the spiral and bring the wire around to form a complete loop.

This version of the doodle dangle necklace has assorted orange-toned glass beads.

Here, free-style doodles are threaded with handmade lampworked beads, suspended on a long black tie cord with a drop bead end detail.

SCALLOPED NECKLACE

Make one, make two or make the scalloped shapes all the way around – it's completely up to you! This necklace design is one of my favourites. If you wish to inject some extra colour, you can create the scallops with different coloured wires. I prefer to stick to silver or gold throughout, because that way I can wear the necklace with everything.

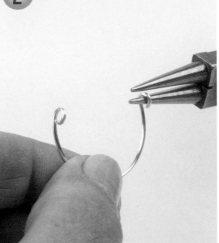

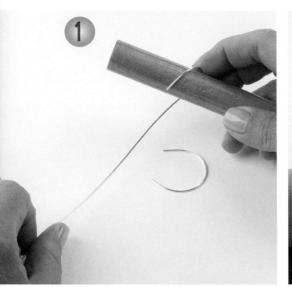

1 Start by creating your centre unit with three to four scalloped shapes. Working from the end of a spool of 1.25mm wire, make 'U' shapes by pushing the wire around different-sized mandrels.

2 Using your round-nosed pliers, create links at each end of the 'U' shapes, forming them at 90 degrees to the frames.

3 Place the 'U' shapes on your steel block and hammer them to spread the rounded ends.

4 Using the dapping end of a hammer, texture the flattened areas.

5 Working from a spool, thead 1mm wire through the right-hand link of the largest 'U' shape, then the right-hand links of the next 'U' shapes in descending order, then a 4mm bead, then a wire coil, then a 4mm bead. Continue, threading on all the left-hand links of the 'U' shapes.

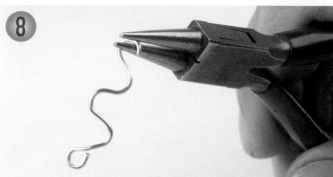

6 Thread on a 6mm bead at either end of the suspended 'U' frames and create a link after each bead using your round-nosed pliers.

7 Repeat to form as many scalloped frames as you wish (enough to go round the whole necklace, or just three for the front). Connect your units to form a chain using jump rings.

8 To create a chain for each side of the scalloped centrepiece, cut ten 5cm (2in) lengths of 1mm wire (or however many you need for the length you desire). Using your round-nosed pliers, create a link, followed by a wiggle in the wire, then another link.

9 Hammer just the wiggle.

10 Repeat to make as many units as you need to go either side of the scalloped section. Connect them using jump rings and add a fish-hook clasp.

Opposite

In this alternative version of the necklace, copper wire adds warmth to the silver.

WIGGLES NECKLACE

It is the use of thick wire that makes this piece dramatic. To keep to the drama, use a strong colour palette with your beads. Alternatively, you can tone it down by wiring in pearl and crystal beads for a more neutral effect. This is a very instant, free-style piece and if you are not used to working in this way, I suggest drawing out your pattern on a piece of paper first and using that as a template.

You will need

0.4mm copper and 2mm orange enamel-coated copper wire

8 x assorted 6–12mm glass beads

Round-, flat- and chain-nosed pliers

Wire cutters

Ring mandrel

Hammer and steel block

1 Cut about 61cm (24in) of 2mm wire and, working from one end, use the widest part of your round-nosed pliers to create a complete loop. Use flat-nosed pliers to turn it into a spiral.

2 As this piece is very free-form and flowing, follow your instincts and curl the wire backwards and forwards into wiggle shapes. You can use the ring mandrel to help you form the larger wiggles. Around the centre of the length, you need to create the largest centrepiece wiggle to keep the design balanced, tapering out to the side wiggles.

3 Spend a little time adjusting the shape, bringing the wiggles together, until you are satisfied. Place the piece on your block and hammer the looped ends of the wiggles, spreading and flattening them. Once the curved areas are flattened, use the dapping head of your hammer to add a little texture. The hammering will misshape it slightly, so readjust as required.

4 Cut a long arm's length of 0.4mm wire and use this to secure your beads in place, within the wiggles. Cut off any excess and neaten the ends.

5 Create a chunky jump ring chain with two different sizes of link (see page 138) made from 2mm orange-coloured wire to connect to each side of the wiggles unit. Make a matching fish hook clasp (see page 141) to secure at the very end.

An orange-coloured wire choker using red beads in assorted sizes, secured with red suede cord and suspended with threaded beads. The cord means this necklace can be worn at variable lengths.

A wiggles bangle. Form the wiggly wire frame around a circular mandrel (a bottle or jar will do) and then secure the beads with wire within some of the spaces.

This version of the necklace has silver and turquoise glass beads with a hand-forged 'S' link chain and clasp. Below is a matching silver and turquoise bangle.

This page and opposite
The orange-coloured wire bangle and choker pieces shown on a model. The choker can be worn at various lengths to suit your outfit.

SCRUNCHED WIRE

With a background in metalwork, I have been inspired to use wire to create solid flat shapes, just like the ones I would pierce out of sheet metal. I am continually fascinated by how tough and durable wire can become when it is hammered and compressed into a solid mass. You cannot hammer one wire over another because this will weaken it, but a mass of scrunched or wrapped wires can become one without the aid of solder.

WIRE AGEING WITHOUT CHEMICALS

If you wish to give your Crescent Moon Choker base (or any of your scrunched pieces) an antiquated look, or add accents of colour to your wires, it is possible to stipple oil-based paints over the wires and then buff them up with wire wool. I would recommend having a practice run on small test pieces first to try out different effects. Experimentation is key!

ORBITAL LINKS

I love creating unusual chains and what I find so pleasing about these orbital links is that even though they are chunky and solid, they are created out of only 0.8mm wire. Make the design your own: you could make all the links the same size, or wire beads into the frames to add colour.

You will need

0.8mm silver-plated copper wire

12 x 10mm blue-dyed faceted quartz beads

2mm (1/8in) cord

Round-, flat- and chain-nosed pliers

Wire cutters

Ring mandrel

Hammer and steel block

1 To create an orbital link, follow steps 1 and 2 of the Sun Scarf Slide project (page 34). Make three large and two small links.

2 Once the ends are tucked in, place each orbital link on your steel block and hammer flat on both sides to compress and work-harden all the wires.

3 Attach the links together with beads and jump rings in between to form an asymmetric chain.

You can choose to bead the whole of the necklace or add cord at the back. If you wish to add cord, cut approximately 18cm (7in) and create cord ends, by wrapping 0.8mm wire around your round-nosed pliers. Slide the ends of the cord into the wire coils and crimp the last coil of each of the coils around the cord to secure. I also add a little dab of superglue by the coil for extra security.

In this version, bronze wire orbital links are connected with threaded burgundy-coloured faceted quartz beads. A brown suede cord completes the look.

This very long necklace features silver wire orbital links in varying diameters, some wired within with glass beads. Matching earrings are created in a similar style.

KNOT CHARM

Inject fun into your pieces with brightly coloured, scrunched-up wires. This technique works well to fill any shaped framework and is much faster than hand weaving.

You will need

Two to three colours of 0.3–0.5mm enamel-coated wire

1mm silver-plated copper wire

Key ring finding

Round-, flat- or chain-nosed pliers

Wire cutters

2.5cm (1in) cylindrical mandrel

Hammer and steel block

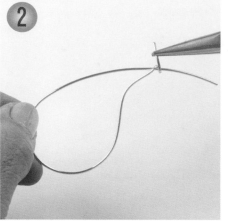

1 Cut approximately 15cm (6in) of 1mm wire and push the centre around a 2.5cm (1in) diameter cylindrical mandrel, creating an inward curve with your fingers to form a paisley shape.

2 Wrap one end of the wire around the other to secure.

3 Using your round-nosed pliers, create a link with the second projecting wire, bringing this end in line with the other, facing the same direction. Trim the ends.

4 Trim the cut ends of the projecting wires and hammer them on a steel block to flatten and spread them. Gently hammer the rest of the outer frame.

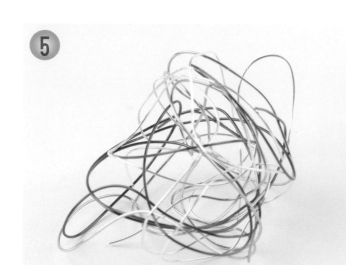

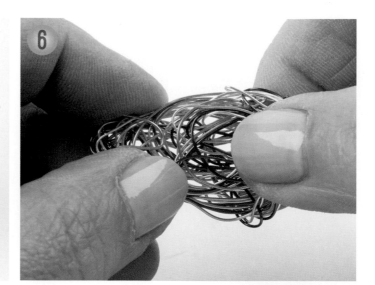

5 Cut two or three arms' lengths of 0.3mm or 0.5mm wire in different colours and scrunch them together with your hands.

6 Roll them into a ball and then tease out to fit the shape of your frame.

7 Cut 30.5cm (12in) of 0.5mm wire and use this to 'sew' the scrunched wire into the space of the frame, securing it around the outer part of the frame as you go.

8 Place the piece on your steel block and gently hammer to flatten the wires within the frame.

9 If you wish to add an embellishment, such as a bead or spiral, wire this onto the frame as desired and then attach the frame to a bag charm clip or key ring finding.

The finished knot charm.

These paisley-shaped charms work well not only as handbag charms and key rings but also as necklaces when attached to chains. Experiment with different coloured wires and beads of your choice.

89

SOLID HEART

As a teacher of wirework jewellery, I know that hearts are one of the most popular motifs. This scrunched heart design is a bold fashion statement and can also look beautiful created as a decoration, suspended from a ribbon.

You will need

0.4mm gold-plated copper wire

0.8mm gold- and silver-plated copper wire

6mm gold bead

Ready-made chain

Round-, flat- and chain-nosed pliers

Wire cutters

2 sizes of circular mandrel

Hammer and steel block

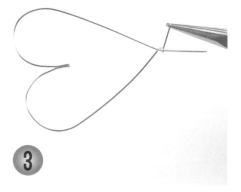

1 You need to create two different-sized heart frames. Cut (8in) of the 0.4mm wire for the inner one and 25.5cm (10in) for the outer. Find the centre of each wire and fold it, pinching at the centre point with your flat-nosed pliers.

2 Use the circular mandrels to create the heart curves; the smaller one for the shorter wire. Bring the wire round the mandrel twice to create the two lobes of the heart.

3 Bring the ends of the wire together and twist them to secure them, creating the point of the frame. Do not cut the wire off yet.

4 Place the smaller heart within the larger frame and use the projecting wire to secure the two together. Again, leave some wire projecting.

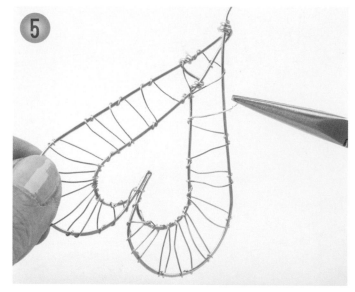

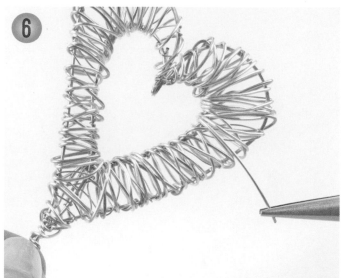

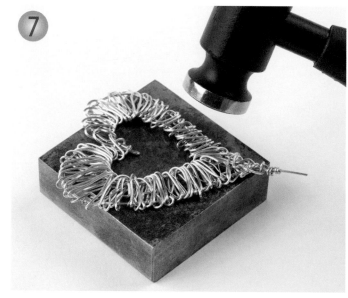

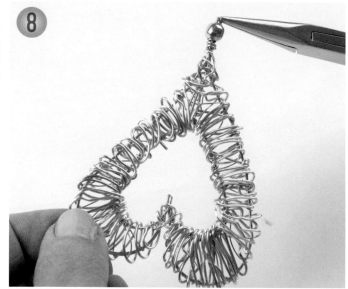

5 Cut an arm's length of 0.4mm gold wire and use this to bind the frames together in a free-style fashion.

6 Cut two further long lengths of 0.8mm gold and silver wire and wrap each one, starting with the gold, around the frame, covering as many gaps as possible. If the wires protrude or look messy, gently tweak or twist them on the frame using the tips of your chain-nosed pliers to tighten them.

7 Place the wire-wrapped heart on your steel block and begin hammering and compressing all the wires together. Increase the blows as you go.

8 Thread a 6mm bead on the projecting wire at the point of the heart and create a headpin (see page 140) to hold it in place.

9 Suspend the heart from two jump rings, one on each side of the frame, pushing the rings through gaps in the binding. Attach a ready-made chain and add a fish-hook clasp.

This small oxidised silver heart pendant is linked to a rose quartz chip and a pearl bead on one side and three hand-forged links (see page 46) on the other. It is suspended from a ready-made silver chain.

The finished Solid Heart.

Cross Pendant

You can use this method to create a variety of pendant shapes. This Cross Pendant was created by making a cross shape base out of 1mm wire and then wire wrapping it with 0.8mm gold and silver wires. The shape was then flattened and compressed with a hammer on a steel block. The projecting hammered wire at the end of the cross was curled into a loop and a freshwater rice pearl was suspended from it.

BASKET MOUNTS

There are endless ways of wire wrapping stones to frame and set them as feature pendants, so I have taken a 'walk on the wild side' and created a backing frame instead, which in turn haloes the stone, making this a really eye-catching piece.

You will need

Two 0.5mm purple, copper and silver enamel-coated coloured wires

0.8mm and 1mm copper wire

Banded agate feature stone

Ready-made chain

Round-, flat- and chain-nosed pliers

Bail-making pliers

Wire cutters

Hammer and steel block

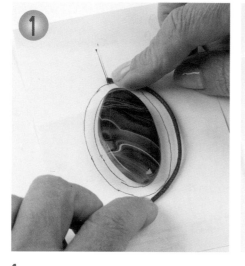

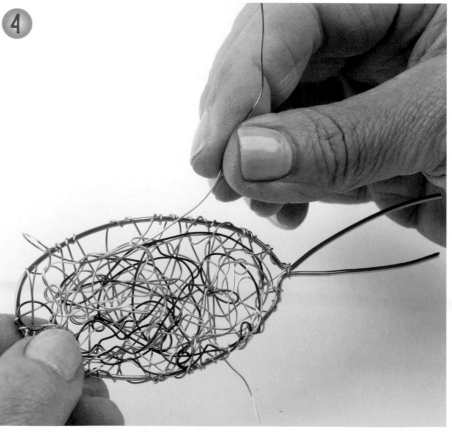

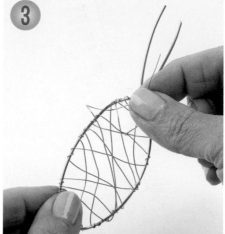

1 Begin by drawing around your stone on a piece of paper. Add about 5mm (1/8in) all round. xMeasure this outline with a piece of string, adding an extra 7.5cm (3in). Cut a length of 1mm wire to that length.

2 Place the centre of the wire on the bottom centre of your drawing and, using your fingers and pliers, bend the wire to fit your drawing frame. Bend the projecting wire upwards at the top as shown.

3 Cut an arm's length of 0.5mm wire and free-style wrap this around the frame. Also wrap around the base of the two projecting wires to hold them together.

4 Cut two further lengths in different colours of 0.5mm wire, this time twice your arm's length, and scrunch them together into a ball. Shape to fit the centre of the frame. Cut an arm's length of 0.5mm wire and 'sew' the scrunched wire into the frame.

5 Use the tips of your chain-nosed pliers to tweak any bulky or loose wires and then place the piece on your steel block to flatten the scrunched wires.

6 Create a bail at the top of the frame by shaping the projecting wires as shown. Cut approximately 35.5cm (12in) of purple 0.5mm wire and wrap the projecting wires, weaving between them as shown.

7 Measure the length of your stone and add 10cm (4in). Cut this length of 0.8mm wire. Thread this wire through your stone with 5cm (2in) projecting at either end.

8 Fold the projecting wires over at right angles and use them to fix the stone to the wire basket frame.

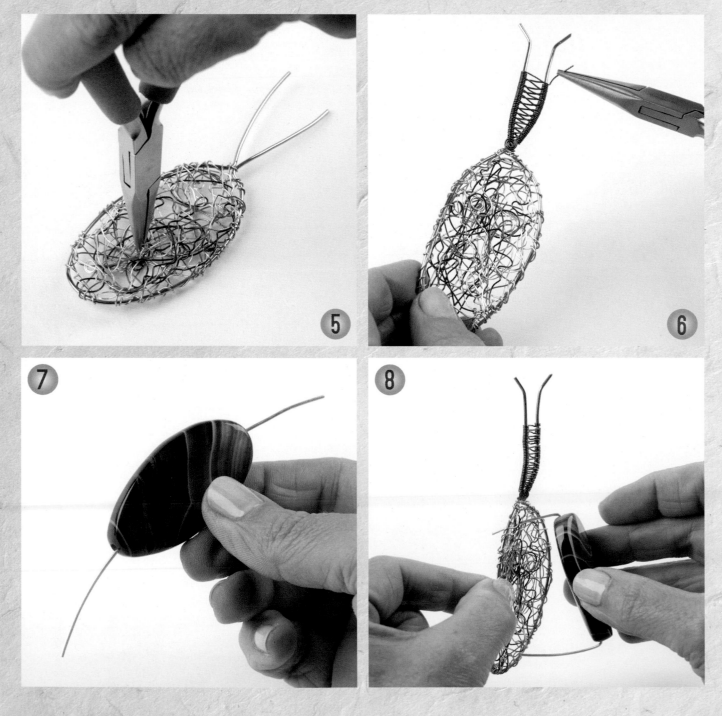

9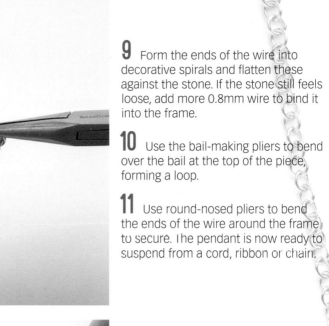

9 Form the ends of the wire into decorative spirals and flatten these against the stone. If the stone still feels loose, add more 0.8mm wire to bind it into the frame.

10 Use the bail-making pliers to bend over the bail at the top of the piece, forming a loop.

11 Use round-nosed pliers to bend the ends of the wire around the frame to secure. The pendant is now ready to suspend from a cord, ribbon or chain.

10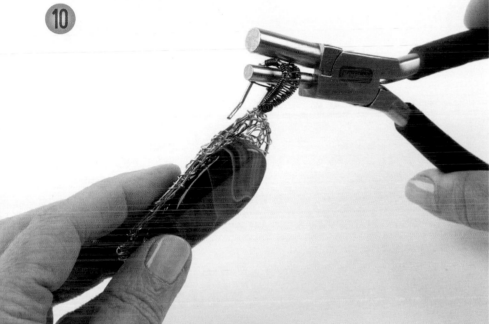

11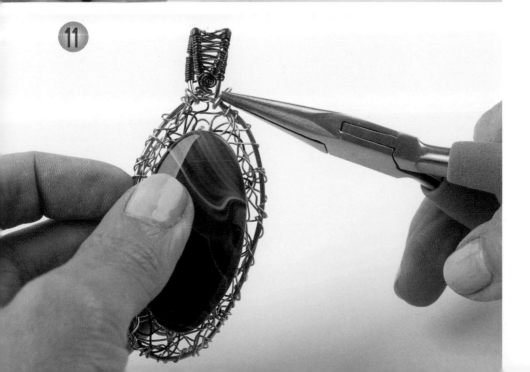

These alternative design basket mounts feature pink and purple banded agate beads, using black and silver wire frames.

Opposite

A pink banded agate stone mounted in a bronze basket frame and scrunched gold and bronze wires. The pendant is suspended from pink cord and bronze chain.

CRESCENT MOON CHOKER

This 'bib' style choker is a fashion piece, and makes a great statement worn either casually or for smart occasions. If you just wish to wrap it with coloured wires and beads and omit the focal stone, this will give you an entirely new look. This technique works equally well created as a bangle frame – check out the Rough Cuff Bangle in the Get Creative chapter (page 126).

You will need

0.6mm silver-plated copper wire

0.8mm and 1.25mm copper wires

Ready-made chain

Oval 18 x 25mm (¾ x 1in) desert agate bead

6 x oval 12mm (½in) carnelian beads

Round-, flat- and chain-nosed pliers

Wire cutters

Large circular mandrel such as a bottle or jar

Hammer and steel block

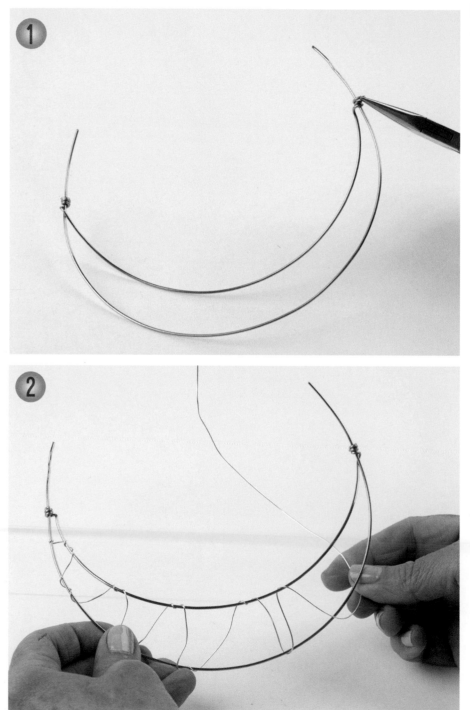

1 To create the crescent-shaped frame, cut one 30.5cm (12in) and one (25.5cm 10in) length of 1.25mm wire. Curve both wires by holding them against a bottle or jar and connect together by wrapping one wire around the other, leaving two ends projecting on each side.

2 Cut a long arm's length of 0.6mm silver wire and use this to randomly wrap around the inside of the frame to provide a bit of solidity before you start wire wrapping with 0.8mm wire.

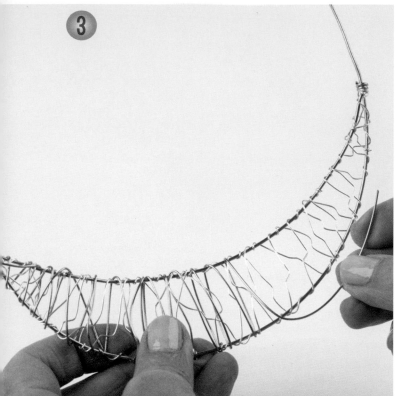

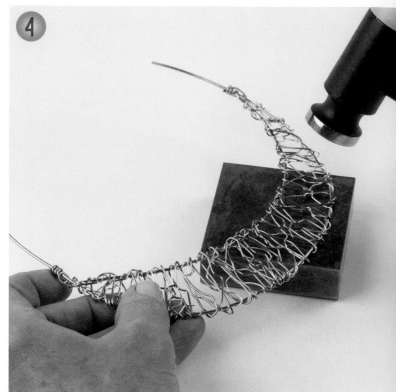

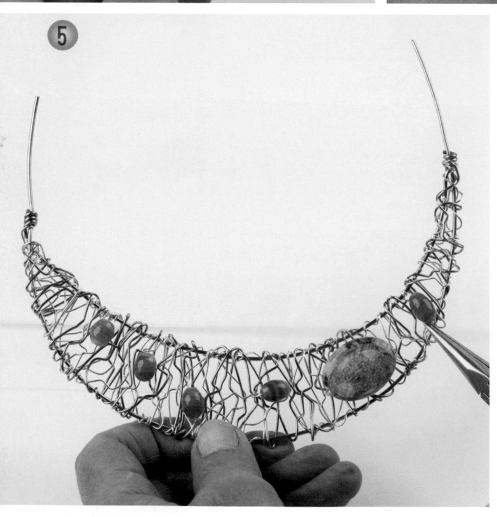

3 Cut two further arms' lengths of 0.8mm wire and wrap these around the frame to fill up the space. If the wires bleed over the sides of the frame, use the tips of your chain-nosed pliers to tweak or bend them in, so that the edges don't end up too messy.

4 Place your crescent frame on a steel block and gently hammer the wires together to compress them, making a solid base.

5 Thread your beads and stone with 0.6mm wire and attach it to the centre or side of the crescent frame.

6 Attach a ready-made chain to each side of the crescent and finish by connecting a fish-hook clasp to the very end. I have added another bead.

Here, silver wire has been dabbed with black and gold oil-based paint to create an oxidised, antique finish. This piece features a greenish-blue cabochon agate stone, mounted asymmetrically.

Opposite
An oval leopard agate cabochon bead set in a bib choker, with silver and brown wires threaded with brown faceted crystals.

GET CREATIVE

This chapter has a mixture of techniques that have been introduced in previous projects. I hope it fuels you with further inspiration and triggers your own imagination. You should discover many permutations for creating timeless, unique designs with wire, beads, pliers and your trusty hammer and block. Let go and express yourself with wire!

CYCLONE PENDANT

Here's another quick make, especially if you have a specialised cone-making tool, or something conical to wrap your wire around! If not, it is possible to use your round-nosed pliers or even a piping nozzle made for icing cakes. These cyclone units can be suspended either way up, as earrings or pendants.

You will need

0.8mm silver-plated copper wire

1 x 4mm white, 2 x 4mm grey, 1 x 6mm grey and 1 x 10mm white pearl beads

Cone-making tool

Round-, flat- and chain-nosed pliers

Wire cutters

Hammer and steel block

1 To make each 'cyclone', cut at least 30.5cm (12in) of 0.8mm wire. Place it on your steel block and hammer it flat along the length, except for about 2.5cm (1in) at either end. This creates a ribbon effect.

2 Wind the ribbon-style wire around your cone-making tool or conical mandrel in a free-style manner.

3 Once all the wire is wound on, tap it with a hammer to work-harden it, then remove it from the cone.

4 Working from a spool, thread 0.8mm wire through the centre of the cone and add your selected beads.

5 Create a headpin (see page 140) at one end and a link at the other.

The finished Cyclone Pendant.

Three different cyclone pendants, threaded with beads in varying ways, created out of silver- and gold-plated wires.

Cyclone earrings with gold and faceted amber glass crystal beads. The cyclone wire shapes are suspended in the opposite way to the step project.

113

FISHBONE EARRINGS

These earrings have the same timeless, tribal feel as the Tribal Feathers Necklace on page 18. A longer matching pendant can also be created by working on a larger scale.

You will need

0.8mm silver-plated copper wire

2 x black seed beads and 2 x 6mm black agate beads

Round-, flat- and chain-nosed pliers

Wire cutters

Hammer and steel block

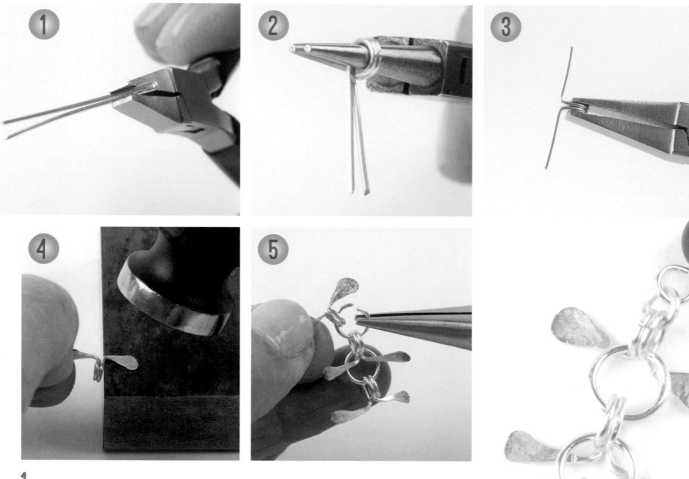

1 Each 'fishbone' will require approximately 5cm (2in) of 0.8mm wire. Find the centre of each length and fold in half, squeezing the wires together with flat-nosed pliers so that they are straight and parallel.

2 Using your round-nosed pliers, create a circular link at the doubled end of the wire.

3 Using the tips of your chain-nosed pliers, bend the projecting wires out in opposite directions at right angles to the link.

4 Using your wire cutters, trim each of the projecting wires to 5mm (1/8in) in length and place the unit on the edge of your steel block to hammer the wires. Spread and flatten the ends into paddle shapes.

5 Create jump rings and connect the fishbone units together in a chain.

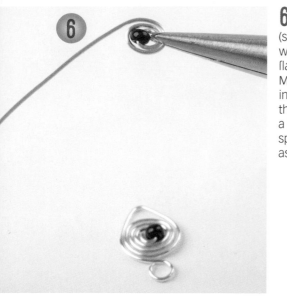

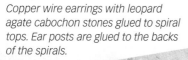

6 Create a headpin with a small bead (see page 140), make a loop at the end with your round-nosed pliers, then use flat-nosed pliers to turn it into a spiral. Make a point as shown to transform it into a fish head shape, and create a link at the other end. Make an earring wire with a larger bead and thread the fishbone unit, spiral fish head and earring wire together as shown.

Copper wire earrings with leopard agate cabochon stones glued to spiral tops. Ear posts are glued to the backs of the spirals.

Gold-plated wire earrings with 3mm blue faceted crystal bead detail.

A silver wire necklace variation on the fishbone theme, suspended with a rose quartz teardrop bead. Chain links are interspersed with rose quartz chip beads and hammer-flattened stalks of wire with a double twist.

HOOPLA SPIRAL EARRINGS

I love simplicity in a design and this piece is no exception, with just a spiral and hoop. Create it in any colour wire you wish, and for a more decorative, colourful piece, you can always fill the centre with beads to create stunning pendants and brooch designs.

You will need

0.4mm and 1mm gold-plated wire

Earring wires

Round-, flat- and chain-nosed pliers

Wire cutters

2.5cm (1in) cylindrical mandrel

Hammer and steel block

1

2

3

4

1 Working from a spool of 1mm wire, use the very tips of your round-nosed pliers to create a tiny curl at the end and use flat-nosed pliers to continue curling the wire around itself to form a tight spiral about 5mm ($^{1}/_{8}$in) in diameter.

2 Position a circular mandrel (to the hoop size desired) next to the tight spiral and bring the wire around the perimeter to create a loop. Cut it off the spool just past the spiral.

3 Secure the cut end around the hoop of wire.

4 Flip the spiral over to hide the cut end.

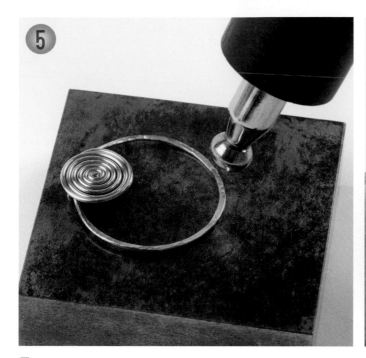

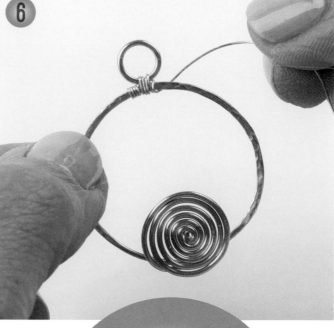

5 Place the hoop on your steel block and flatten and spread the circular frame, leaving the spiral untouched. Use the dapping head of your hammer to create texture.

6 Cut approximately 7.5cm (3in) of 0.4mm wire and secure a jump ring at the opposite end of the hoop, ready to suspend from an earring wire. Repeat all of the steps above to create a pair.

Tip

For a 3D effect, use the tips of your round-nosed pliers to push the back of the spiral coils out.

The finished earrings.

Silver wire earrings with blue spirals glued to the centres and a blue wire coil detail on the earring wires.

120

Create a matching pendant for your earrings, following all the project steps, then wire in some beads with 0.4mm gold wire. I have used freshwater pearls, gold beads and glass amber crystals to fill the centre space and suspended the pendant from a gold chain.

CLEO'S EARRINGS

Checking back to Cleopatra's Collar necklace on page 50, you will find that these earrings make a great match! Alternatively, use thicker gauge wire and increase the loops to make a statement pendant. This design can be suspended either way up, tapering or flaring out at the ends. I personally prefer the elegance of the taper, but have fun suspending it either way!

You will need

0.4mm and 0.8mm silver-plated copper wire
4 x 4mm Czech glass crystal beads
Two fish-hook earring wires
Round-, flat- and chain-nosed pliers
Wire cutters
Hammer and steel block

1 Make three wiggles from 0.8mm wire as shown.

2 Cut 10cm (4in) of 0.8mm wire. Find the centre and cross the wires over to form a loop.

3 Create links on the ends with round-nosed pliers and spiral them towards the central loop.

4 Hammer the curves of all the loops and the spirals, but avoid the crossed-over wires or you will weaken them.

5 In the single wiggle, bind in a bead to match the necklace using 0.4mm wire.

6 Connect the three units using jump rings on either side as shown. Attach to an earring wire with another bead and repeat to make a pair.

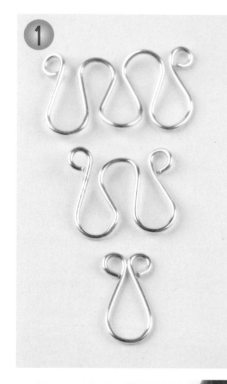

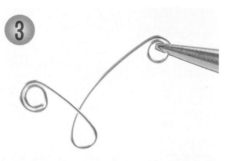

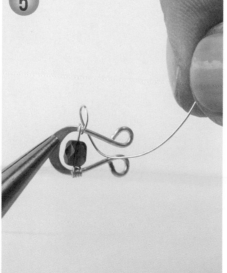

Opposite

Cleo's Earrings make a perfect jewellery set, twinned with Cleopatra's Collar from page 50.

Left: Gold wire wiggle units connected the other way up from the main project and suspended with faceted rondelle crystal beads.

Right: Copper wire earrings suspended with a green oval bead decoration.

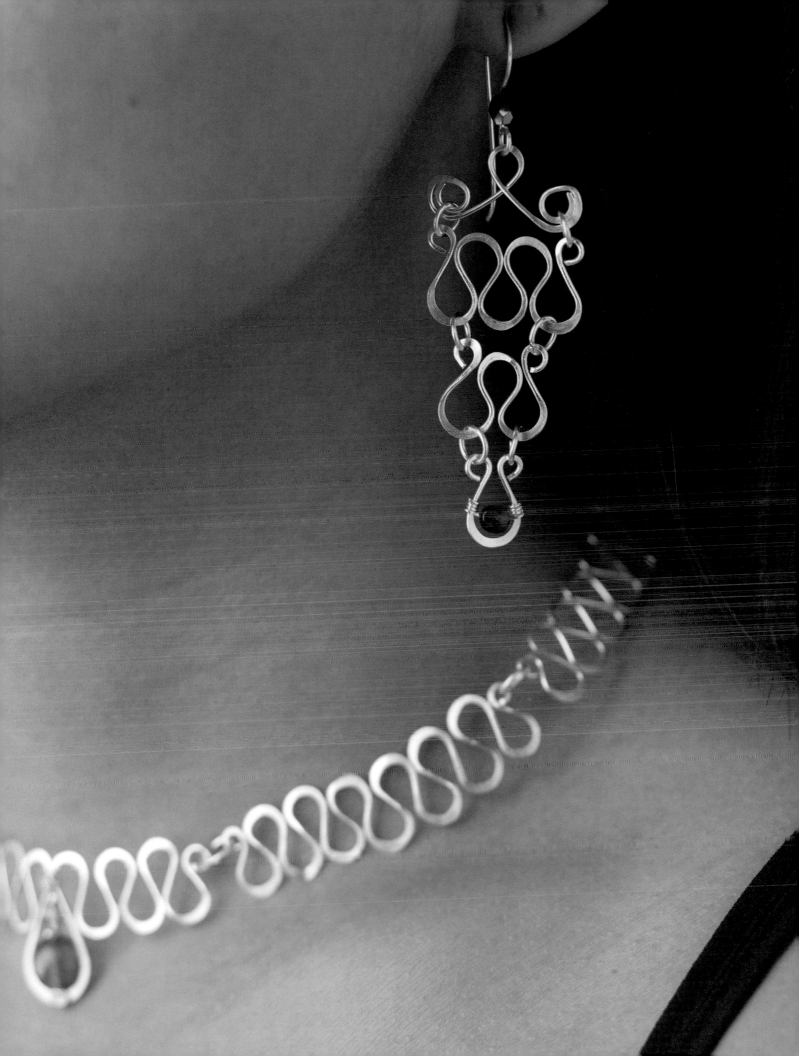

ROUGH CUFF BANGLE

This form of wire compression creates large shapes and can be used to make all types of jewellery designs. This bangle will hopefully inspire you to jump in and experiment with other shapes for rings, brooches and pendants.

You will need

0.6mm and 1.25mm copper wires

0.5mm coloured enamel-coated wires in red, gold and green

Round-, flat- and chain-nosed pliers

Wire cutters

Cylindrical mandrel

Hammer and steel block

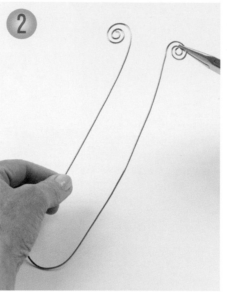

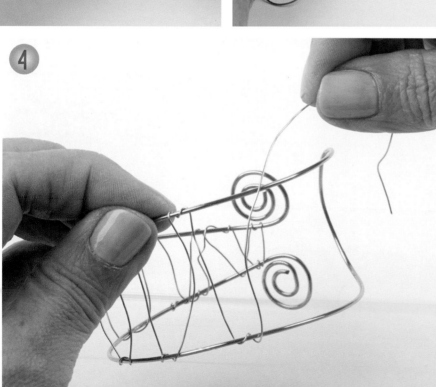

1 Cut approximately 56cm (22in) of 1.25mm wire and bend the centre around a cylindrical mandrel of about 2.5cm (1in) or to the desired bangle width.

2 Create spirals at the very ends of the wires, curling them outwards.

3 Place around a circular frame such as a rolling pin to shape into a bangle

4 Once you're happy with the shape, cut an arm's length of 0.6mm wire and use this to free-style wrap the inner part of the bangle, wrapping it round each side of the frame as you go.

5 Cut a long arm's length of three different 0.5mm coloured wires (I used red, gold and green) and begin randomly wrapping the frame, filling the space. When you run out of wire, cut another length in a different colour and continue until you have filled the frame. Using the tips of your chain-nosed pliers, twist and tweak any stray wires to tighten them around the frame and add a little interest.

6 Place the bangle around your cylindrical mandrel and gently stroke hammer the wires flat to compress and toughen them.

The finished bangle.

A silver wire cuff with semi-precious chip beads, attached to the frame with 0.4mm silver wire.

This version of the bangle has a black aluminium 2mm wire frame, with 0.4mm silver and black scrunched wires attached and wired on (as in step 4 and 5 of the Basket Mount project on pages 96 and 98).

Silver and gold wire cuffs, with beaded and wire shaped details.

ARROW HEADS

As wire lends itself to rounded ends and curls, I felt it was important to show that it is also possible to add a sharper edge or spike to your designs. These arrow heads started life as a magazine project about mimicking bunting flags!

You will need

0.8mm copper wire
Round-, flat- and chain-nosed pliers
Wire cutters
Earring wires
2 x 3mm copper beads
4 x rose quartz chip beads
Hammer and steel block

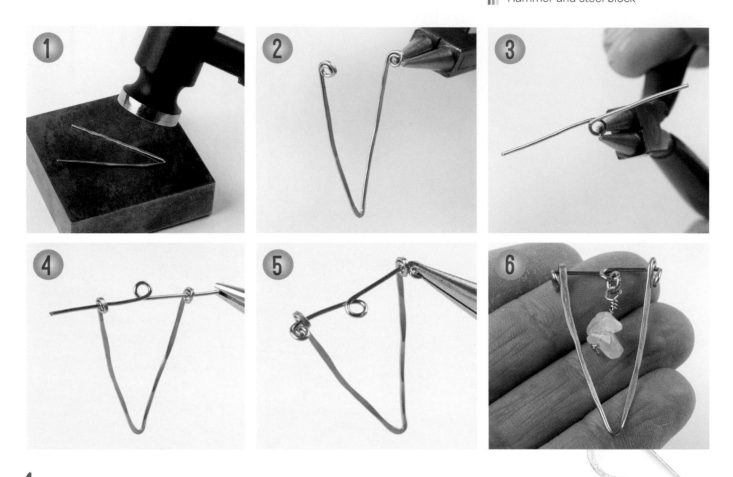

1 For each 'arrow tip', cut 7.5cm (3in) of 0.8mm wire. Find the centre and bend in half. Squeeze the folded part with flat-nosed pliers, then open out into a 'V' shape. Place this on your steel block and hammer to flatten.

2 Use the tips of your round-nosed pliers to curl the very ends into small links, keeping them at 90 degrees to the frame.

3 Cut approximately 5cm (2in) of 0.8mm wire and place your round-nosed pliers at the centre. Bring the wires around until they cross over in opposite directions, creating a link at the centre.

4 Thread both ends through the top links of the 'V' unit, positioning the link at the centre of the frame.

5 Create a small tight spiral at either end of the horizontal wire to secure it in place.

6 Suspend a linked bead at the centre, using jump rings as shown. Attach an earring wire. Repeat all the steps to make two earrings.

Silver wire arrow heads linked as a chain to form a necklace, with malachite chip beads.

A black iron wire necklace with purple faceted crystal beads and black chain. The matching earrings have spiral tops with ready-made earring posts glued on the reverse.

ORBITAL RINGS

This scrunched, compressed wire technique is not only great for creating chunky statement chain links (as in the Scrunched Wire collection); it is also a quick and very effective way of creating ring shanks. Just hammer the wire in a different way to create the orbital ring and the shank.

You will need

0.4mm and 0.8mm gold-plated wire
12 x 2mm pearl beads
Amethyst nugget bead
Round-, flat- and chain-nosed pliers
Wire cutters
Ring mandrel
2.5cm (1in) cylindrical mandrel
Hammer and steel block

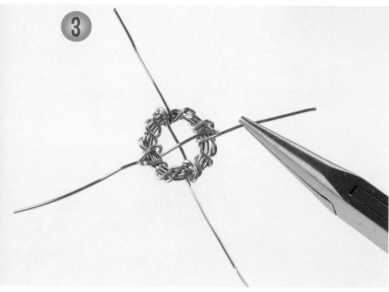

1 To create the three scrunched circles of wire (one for the shank and two for the front of the ring), follow steps 1 – 4 of the 'Orbital Links' project on page 82. The smaller front ring can be made by wrapping wire around the narrow end of a ring mandrel and the largest circle by wrapping around a 2.5cm (1in) cylindrical mandrel.

2 Hammer the two circles for the front of the ring, but not the one for the shank.

3 Cut two 15cm (6in) lengths of 0.8mm wire. Wrap these crosswise around the edges of the smaller circle as shown.

4 Use the projecting wires to attach the larger circle, wrapping the wires around its edges. Trim and neaten the wire ends.

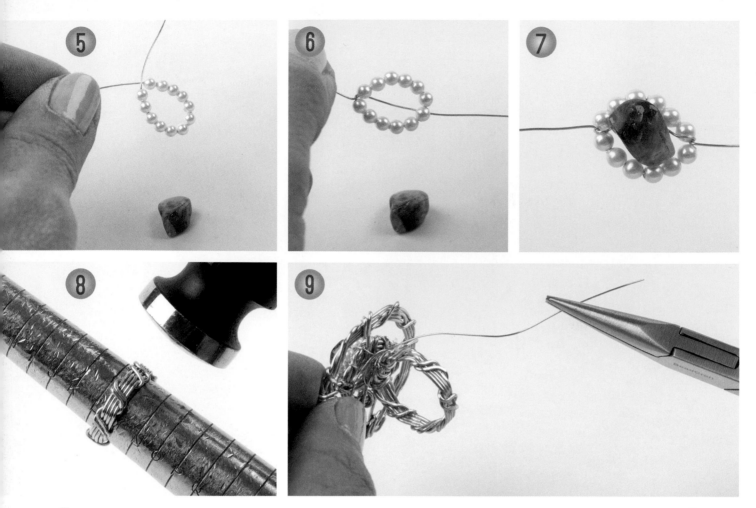

5 Cut 12.7cm (5in) of 0.4mm wire and thread on enough small pearl beads to form a loop around your chosen focal bead.

6 Cross the wires over and bring one down through the centre of the beaded loop.

7 Thread on the focal bead, pushing it into the centre of the loop. To secure it, bring the wire round the edge of the loop and pull it. Secure this beaded piece to the centre of the orbital link frame using the remaining wire.

8 To make the ring shank, use the remaining orbital ring and hammer it on a ring mandrel instead of on a steel block.

9 Cut more 0.4mm wire and use it to attach the shank to the orbital rings.

The finished ring.

Opposite

These large rings make a striking statement but they are surprisingly easy to wear.

Below, centre

A two-tone, gold and silver wire ring with semi-precious chip beads (carnelian, amethyst, rose quartz and peridot).

Below, right

A bronze wire ring with an aquamarine bead.

BASIC TECHNIQUES

MAKING JUMP RINGS

Even though these are readily available to purchase from jewellery suppliers, creating your own means you can match the rings to the colour and size of wire that you are using, not to mention the money you will save! Jump rings can be linked together to form chains, or used as connectors for beads, charms and chains.

You'll be amazed at how simple jump rings are to make, just by forming an even-sized coil around the shaft of your round-nosed pliers (or any circular mandrel such as a pen or chunky knitting needle) to the diameter you require.

Tip

Always open the links sideways – like a door – so that you do not distort the shape.

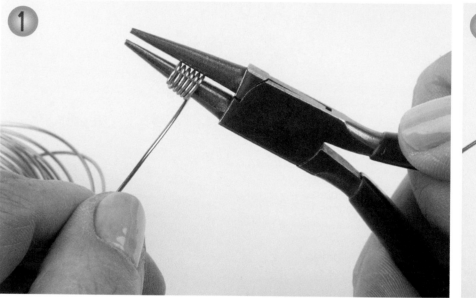

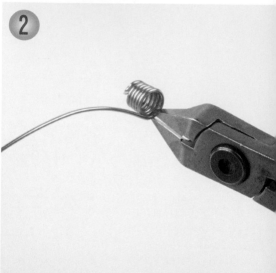

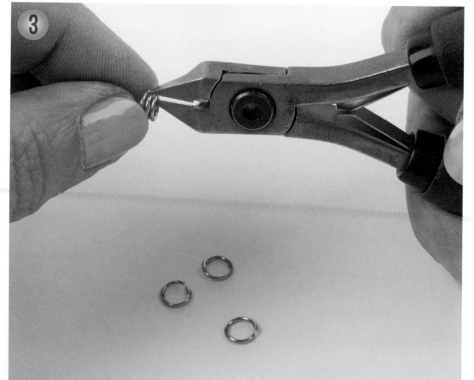

1 Working from a spool, wrap the wire six to eight times around one shaft of your round-nosed pliers, making sure the second ring of the coil is formed just beside the first. Keep the wire coiling around on the same part of the pliers to ensure the coil stays even.

2 Remove the tight coil from the pliers and cut it off from the spool using the tips of your wire cutters.

3 Find the cut end and using your wire cutters, snip upward into the next ring of the coil above, thereby cutting off a full circle. Continue cutting each ring off the coil in turn to obtain more jump rings.

MAKING BEAD LINKS

A bead link is just a bead threaded onto a wire with a neat circle formed at either end in order for the bead to be suspended or connected.

1 Thread your chosen bead onto a spool of wire, leaving approximately 1cm (½in) of wire extending.

2 Hold the bead vertically on the wire and using the very tips of your round-nosed pliers, bend the wire at a right angle, at the point where it touches the bead.

3 Hold and squeeze the very end of the bent wire in your round-nosed pliers and curl it around to form a small circle, following the contour of your pliers. Try not to do this in one swift movement, but rather in several short manipulations, repositioning the pliers as necessary.

4 Cut the wire from the spool, leaving approximately 1cm (½in) projecting at the opposite end of the bead, and repeat steps 2–3 to form another link at the other end of the bead.

5 Once you have made a link on either side of the bead, hold them firmly in your flat- and chain-nosed pliers and twist until both links are on the same plane.

MAKING A HEADPIN

If you wish to suspend beads from chains (like charms) or create bead drop earrings, you will only need to create a link at one end of the bead and a headpin at the other, to prevent the bead from sliding off the wire. The simplest headpin should be virtually invisible and is a doubled-up tip to the wire. However, you can be very imaginative and create spirals, freeform shapes or hammered ends.

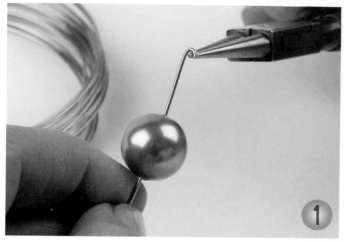

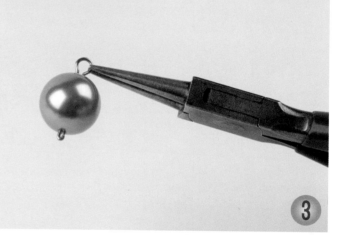

1 Working from a spool, thread your chosen bead onto the wire and let it slip down, leaving the end exposed. Using the very tips of your chain- or round-nosed pliers, create a tiny hook at the very end.

2 Using the tips of your chain- or flat-nosed pliers, squeeze the hook to create a knob of doubled wire.

3 Push your bead right up to the knob of wire and check it doesn't slip off (if it does, bend the knob 90 degrees, like a shelf for it to sit on). Cut the wire from the spool, leaving a stem of about 1cm (½in) and use this to form a link with your round-nosed pliers.

Tip

If your doubled wire end is too long at step 2, you can always cut through one of the wires to remove and shorten the overall length of the headpin.

This bracelet shows a few different headpin styles. From left to right: standard (as in the steps above); closed spiral; flattened spiral; 'Greek key' and hammered 'feather' tip (step 2, page 18).

MAKING A FISH-HOOK CLASP

This is probably the most common wire clasp and also one of the simplest to create. Once you have mastered the basic technique, you can experiment with altering the shape to blend with different designs.

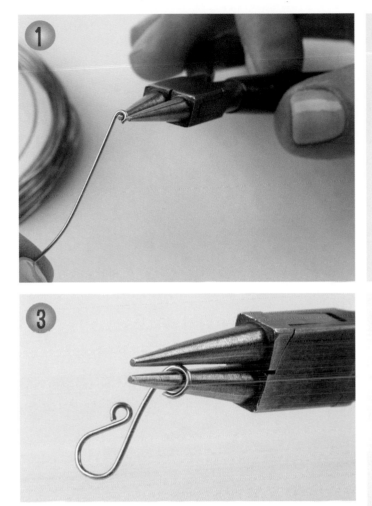

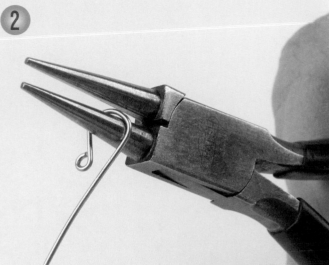

1 Working directly from a spool of wire, curl the end into a tiny loop using round-nosed pliers.

2 Reposition the wider part of your round-nosed pliers on the other side of the wire, just under the loop and curl the wire in the opposite direction to form the 'hook' of the clasp.

3 Cut the wire off the spool, leaving about 1cm (½in), and form a link at the opposite end.

4 Place the hook on your steel block and gently 'stroke' hammer the rounded end to flatten and spread it, thereby work-hardening it.

MAKING THE 'EYE' OF THE FASTENER

This is primarily a wrapped link, but is more durable than using a jump ring, which could open or distort due to wear and tear.

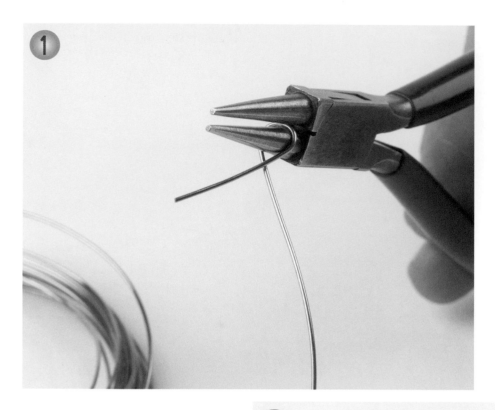

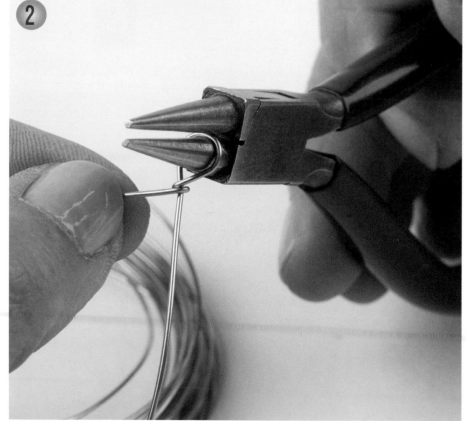

1 Working from a spool of wire, place the widest part of your round-nosed pliers about 2.5cm (1in) from the end and curl the wire around to form a loop, crossing the end of the wire over itself.

2 Wrap the extending wire around the stem, just under the loop, to secure it.

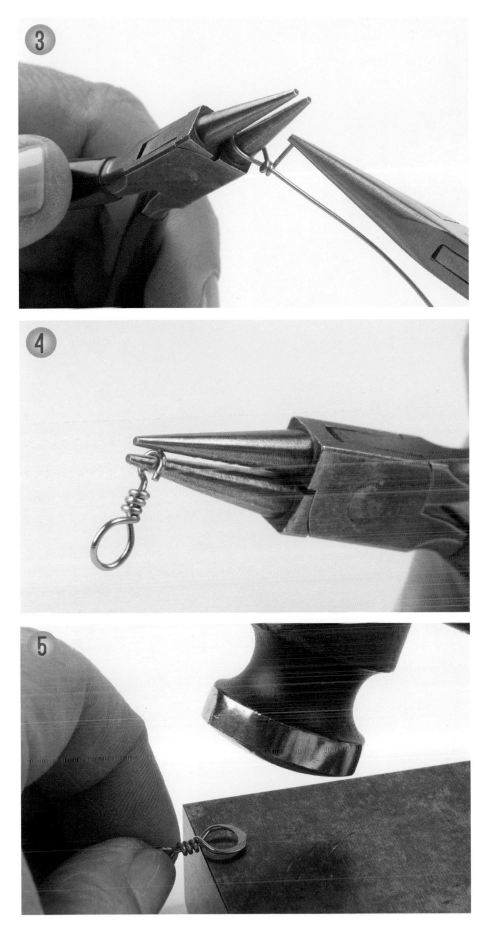

3 Continue with a couple more tight wraps around the stem and cut from the spool. Use the very tips of your chain-nosed pliers to neaten the cut end and flatten it against the stem wire.

4 Cut the stem wire from the spool, leaving approximately 1cm (½in), and use this to create a link with your round-nosed pliers.

5 Place the wrapped 'eye' loop on your steel block and gently 'stroke' hammer the outer edge of the loop to flatten and work-harden it.

Tip
Don't hammer the wrapped wires on the stem, as you will weaken them.

INDEX